lonely planet

THE CRUISE HANDBOOK

Inspiring ideas and essential advice for the new generation of cruises and cruisers

CONTENTS

SMOOTH SAILING

PLANNING

INSPIRATION

CHOOSE YOUR CRUISE

SMOOTH

SAILING

WHY CRUISE?

Tell a random selection of people that you're going on a cruise, and we guarantee you'll get a mixed bag of responses. Some will coo with jealousy; others will recoil with disgust. There's no travel category as polarising as the cruise, but actually, this is one form of travel that can accommodate all comers. Today, destinations are more diverse than ever, onboard food and entertainment have reached new heights and the average cruiser keeps getting younger. Still, the traditional image of a cruise vacation remains outdated. This book aims to refresh those stale perceptions. We'll cover everything from full-on leisure to nonstop action to show you how cruises today are as diverse as the destinations they unlock and as varied as the vacationers they attract. With industry figures indicating that 27.2 million passengers embark on cruises annually, to dismiss them is to lose out on a range of great experiences.

So, is a cruise right for you, and if so, what type? Maybe you're looking to get away from the daily grind and have someone else deal with the cleaning and cooking. The staff on an all-inclusive cruise is as close to a genie in a lamp as it gets, while cruises outclass typical land resorts with their assortment of dining and activity options. On an oceangoing megaship,

would you like dim sum or pancakes for breakfast? Tacos or sushi for lunch? You can watch a Broadway-style show, go ice skating or try to Escape the Room after dinner. Or if it's peace you're after, just unwind poolside and have the sun melt away your cares. That's the beauty of cruise travel.

On the other hand, if the idea of "unwinding poolside" sends shivers of boredom down your spine? Don't run screaming from cruising because of that. A cruise can reach landscapes and cultures that are inaccessible by airplane or car – remote destinations of untouched beauty like the distant fjords of Norway or the interior river systems of Southeast Asia.

What's more, with cruising, you don't have to restrict yourself to only one type of travel. You can take one holiday that's deeply immersive and culturally enriching, and then opt to completely unplug your brain and lie in the sun on the next one. Heck, a single trip can even mix and match modes. In fact, a vacation that dabbles in a bit of both will likely be the perfect recipe to ease the stresses of daily life. Want to spend your days hiking ancient trails or scouring contemporary art galleries, then retreat to a relaxing all-inclusive dinner only footsteps away from your bed? A cruise might be the glass slipper you're missing.

A BRIEF HISTORY OF ADVENTURE

Cruising brings you into communion with one of the most ancient modes of transit. The annals of human history are filled with daring passages across the world's oceans that make Vasco da Gama's voyage seem like nothing more than a splash in the bathtub.

Carbon dating suggests that ancient humans were crafting seafaring tools from stone as early as 130,000 BC. Things really picked up around 4000 BC when Greeks, Egyptians and Chinese began sailing the seas in earnest. The Polynesians, too, settled the quiet recesses of the South Pacific at this time.

By around 600 BC the Phoenicians had become master seafarers, setting up colonies all over the Mediterranean and exploring the waters around England, the Red Sea and the Indian Ocean. While the rise and fall of the Roman Empire led to centuries of the Dark Ages in Europe, the Vikings were busy charting new continents with their voyages beyond Iceland, Greenland and eventually

10

ESSENTIAL FILMS
SET AT SEA

Titanic (1997)
Finding Nemo (2003)
The Poseidon Adventure (1972)
Pirates of the Caribbean (2003)
The Life Aquatic (2004)
Cast Away (2000)
Jaws (1975)
Captain Ron (1992)
The Little Mermaid (1989)
Gentlemen Prefer Blondes (1953)

Canada's Newfoundland in 1000 AD – about 500 years before John Cabot discovered the continent of North America.

Exploration of the Americas and new, streamlined trade routes turned European kingdoms into outright colonialists. Portugal and Spain launched their surveying ships around the African continent to Asia and the Americas all by the end of the 15th century. England and France soon joined the race, and by the end of the 18th century

land grabs had conquered and laid claim to significant portions of the globe in the name of their respective royals. The consequences of their actions continue to shape the world we see today in almost every way.

After the Industrial Revolution in the first half of the 19th century, leisure cruising came into being when the idea of vacationing became a viable pursuit for the newly emerging middle class. The British-based Peninsular & Oriental Steam

Navigation Company (which
you might know as P&O today)
paired cargo shipping with
passenger ferrying throughout the
Mediterranean. Soon a cluster
of ships offered transatlantic
passages to North America. By the
early 20th century, it was possible
to cross the ocean in style – with
the ill-fated *Titanic* being the most
famous example of early cruising
opulence. Later, author Agatha
Christie made a leisurely holiday
cruise in Egypt the set piece for
her novel *Death on the Nile*.

The advent of commercial
travel by airplane quickly crushed
the cruising industry in the
1960s, although the popular '70s
television show *The Love Boat*
made ocean travel seem like a
desirable pursuit for couples.
In the '80s a new fleet of ships
emerged, sprouting amenities
like pool decks and shuffleboard,
and soon thereafter megaships
morphed into floating cities – the
type David Foster Wallace wrote
about in his essay "A Supposedly
Fun Thing I'll Never Do Again."
Since then the stuffy old cruise
liner experience has had a major
refresh, but any vessel you take
will be following a tradition of
seafaring laid out centuries upon
centuries ago.

10 ESSENTIAL READS INVOLVING TRAVEL BY BOAT

The Odyssey by Homer
The Tempest by William Shakespeare
Mutiny on the Bounty by Charles Nordhoff and James Norman Hall
We, the Drowned by Carsten Jensen
In the Heart of the Sea by Nathaniel Philbrick
The Old Man and the Sea by Ernest Hemingway
Moby-Dick by Herman Melville
Twenty-Thousand Leagues Under the Sea by Jules Verne
Treasure Island by Robert Louis Stevenson
Life of Pi by Yann Martel

5 PATH-BREAKING EXPLORERS YOU SHOULD KNOW

Vasco da Gama

1. Gudridur Thorbjarnardottir
Norse explorer Gudridur
gave birth to the first
child of European
descent on the North
American continent
around 1000 AD. After
returning to her native
Iceland, she headed
to Rome to relate her
travels to the pope.

2. Vasco da Gama
Portuguese explorer
da Gama lays claim to
being the first European
navigator to find a sea
route to India, during a
voyage spanning from
1497 to 1499.

3. Ferdinand Magellan
A Portuguese explorer
working for the Spanish
crown, Magellan was
the first European
navigator to cross the
Pacific, in 1520.

4. Abel Tasman
A Dutch explorer
working for the
profiteering Dutch
East India Company,
in 1642 Tasman was
the first European
to make landfall on
what is now Tasmania
(named after him,
though originally
called Van Diemen's
Land) and to sight
New Zealand.

5. James Cook
Cook's three voyages
explored most of
the corners of the
South Pacific. From
1768 until his death
in Hawaii he
mapped the edges of
New Zealand and
became the first
European to sail
Australia's east coast.

THE CRUISE HANDBOOK

DEBUNKING THE UNCOOL CRUISE MYTH

Despite the huge sea change in the cruising industry that's left stereotypes hopelessly outdated, misconceptions persist. If you've ever found yourself offering any of these opinions, it may be time for a reality check.

"CRUISES DON'T GET TO THE HEART OF A DESTINATION."

Sure, weeklong itineraries stopping at a different Caribbean port every day may not be going deep – but that's exactly their intention. These cruises are designed to prioritise fun, whether that's lounging on a private beach under the warm tropical sun, or staying up into the wee hours of the night enjoying musicals, comedy shows, club DJs and live bands. At the other end of the spectrum, however, there are cruises that deliver authenticity, with smaller boats that reach up close and personal to a location. These attract a demographic of traveller that is looking to profoundly engage in the region of their choice. Whatever type of travel you prefer, there is a cruise to match.

"CRUISES ATTRACT ONLY A CERTAIN TYPE OF PERSON, AND THAT'S NOT ME."

If one cruise experience doesn't interest you, another one out there surely will. Each cruise attracts different types of people from around the globe, and there's no need to go on a one-size-fits-all cruise when so many tailored options exist. For example, science and expedition vessels – even cargo ships – appeal to travellers with an appetite for adventure, accessing some of the most remote corners of the globe. For those who prefer a more social scene, increasing numbers of cruise lines have millennial-only cruises tailored to young travellers hoping to make friends and connect to people. Or perhaps you'd prefer to create your own adventure. Try a hand at self-chartering a boat and make the world your oyster.

"CRUISES ARE TOO EXPENSIVE."

Think that low prices for an all-inclusive cruise are too good to be true? Thanks to websites like Cruise Critic (www.cruisecritic.com), you can easily check what is and isn't included in your potential trip before you book your ticket. With transit, lodging and food all covered, a cruise is often a much better value than a vacation on land, especially if you book off-season and avoid extras on board like alcohol. In general the competition between brands ensures excellent value for money. Large cruising companies want nothing more than your repeat business and will reward you in kind for your loyalty.

"CRUISES HAVE GENERIC, UNEXCITING FOOD."

Cruise companies have stepped up their game when it comes to dining; even megaships have fallen under the foodie sway of culinary tourism. Larger cruise ships offer a variety of specialty restaurants, while smaller river cruises offer cooking classes and trips to regional markets. Small boats are especially good at connecting travellers to refined versions of local specialties.

THE CRUISE HANDBOOK

CRUISING CATEGORIES

*Still not sure what your cruise options really look like?
Here's a quick overview of the different types of cruising.*

MEGASHIPS

It's not so much about the destination as it is about the panoply of amenities on board. These aren't mere cruises – they're floating cities stocked with every entertainment under the sun. The competition in this category is fierce, as cruise lines crack a bottle of champagne over new and improved vessels at a rapid pace. Some megaship cruise lines include, but are not limited to:

Royal Caribbean International
(www.royalcaribbean.com)
Norwegian Cruise Line
(www.ncl.com)
Celebrity Cruises
(www.celebritycruises.com)
Princess Cruises
(www.princess.com)
Carnival Cruise Line
(www.carnival.com)
Holland America Line
(www.hollandamerica.com)
MSC Cruises
(www.msccruisesusa.com)
Disney Cruise Line
(disneycruise.disney.go.com)

LUXURY VESSELS

These luxury lines promise a palpable uptick in service across the board. From small 100-person ships with sails to large 1000-person cruisers that feel more like floating five-star hotels, opulence and exclusivity are the major draw. Expect sweet suites and perks on board. Some luxury lines include:

Crystal Cruises
(www.crystalcruises.com)
Seabourn Cruise Line
(www.seabourn.com)
Silversea Cruises
(www.silversea.com)
Regent Seven Seas Cruises
(www.rssc.com)
Oceania Cruises
(www.oceaniacruises.com)
Cunard Line *(www.cunard.com)*

Viking Cruises
(www.vikingcruises.com)
Windstar Cruises
(www.windstarcruises.com)

EXPEDITION CRUISES

Explore the world on these multipurpose vessels that mix the excitement of discovery with active excursions and onboard lectures. These ships chart the waters of some of the most far-flung regions of the globe, and do so in style. Some expedition lines include, but are not limited to:

Hurtigruten
(www.hurtigruten.com)
Lindblad Expeditions
(www.expeditions.com)
Quark Expeditions
(www.quarkexpeditions.com)
Peregrine Adventures
(www.peregrineadventures.com)
UnCruise Adventures
(www.uncruise.com)
Aranui Cruises
(www.aranui.com)

RIVER CRUISES

The world's rivers have been connecting people for centuries, and today's river cruises prioritise exploring the rich culture onshore without lacking amenities on board. Itineraries have expanded beyond the more traditional European destinations to include rivers throughout the world, from Asia and Africa to the Americas.

Clockwise from left: The restaurant on a U by Uniworld river cruise; a Viking infinity pool; a Silversea cruise; the lounge on Viking *Sea*

Some river cruise lines include, but are not limited to:
Avalon Waterways
(www.avalonwaterways.com)
Uniworld Boutique River Cruise Collection
(www.uniworld.com)
AmaWaterways
(www.amawaterways.com)
Tauck *(www.tauck.com)*
Pandaw River Cruises
(www.pandaw.com)
Grand Circle Cruise Line
(www.gct.com)
Aqua Expeditions
(www.aquaexpeditions.com)
Viking River Cruises
(www.vikingrivercruises.com)

CHARTER CRUISES

If the thought of cruising with multitudes of other passengers doesn't appeal, consider chartering your own boat with or without a crew. Vessels are available for all wallet sizes and levels of experience, from river barges to cove-to-cove island hoppers. Self-charter cruise options include, but are not limited to:
The Moorings
(www.moorings.com)
The Yacht Week
(www.theyachtweek.com)
Nicholson Yacht Charters
(www.yachtvacations.com)
Sailo *(www.sailo.com)*

CRUISING: THE NUMBERS

- The Cruise Lines International Association (CLIA) has over 50 cruise line members.

- Over 27 million people took a cruise in 2018.

- Sailings in the Caribbean represents over 35% of the entire market.

- Americans comprise roughly half of cruisers worldwide.

- Chinese cruisers are the second-largest group (over 2 million); German and British travellers rank third and fourth.

- The cruise industry employs over 1.1 million people.

SUSTAINABILITY

With the Great Pacific garbage patch growing each year and the coral reefs suffering worldwide from bleaching events, vacationers increasingly want to know if their cruises are further harming the ocean environment. Most cruise companies, both big and small, are cognizant that their essential resource, clean water, is in peril.

As a result, reducing onboard waste and enacting ship-wide recycling programs are the focus of major initiatives in the industry, with some brands like Royal Caribbean International even pledging to eliminate the use of single-use straws. Exhaust gas cleaning systems called scrubbers are being installed on most Carnival Cruise ships, but are

not yet the industry standard.

The most ecologically responsible cruises are ships powered by the wind instead of diesel engines; beyond the release of unwelcome fuels, the noise pollution created by large ships is an extremely problematic disruption for marine animals like dolphins and whales who use echolocation in order to navigate

1. BRING YOUR OWN WATER BOTTLE. Whether walking around the ship or getting off to explore your surroundings, stay away from plastic water bottles and opt for a light, reusable water bottle from home.

2. DON'T USE PLASTIC BAGS. On beach-centric cruises you're certain to have a wet bathing suit at an inopportune time – bring a small washable and reusable bag to store it in instead of opting for a single-use plastic bag.

3. TAKE ACTION. Ask your operator of choice if they partner with any oceanographic initiatives – maybe volunteer opportunities will be available while you sail. Crystal Cruises, for example, runs a "You Care, We Care" program for beach cleanups, tree planting and animal rescues.

4. SAIL OUT OF A NEARBY PORT. Avoiding flying to your cruise port helps minimise your vacation emissions. Drive or take public transit to the port instead.

5. DONATE TO CHARITY. You can always add a carbon offset donation to your travel budget to balance out your environmental impact. These charities invest in clean-energy projects and fight deforestation.

the sea. (Most larger ships must rely on engines to keep on schedule, however.) Hurtigruten's MS *Roald Amundsen*, which launched in 2018, is one of the greenest larger vessels on the high seas, with a state-of-the-art hybrid engine functioning predominantly on battery. Ports are starting to prioritise access to shore power as well, which generates less of a footprint.

Though they no longer work with the CLIA, the nonprofit Friends of the Earth has an archive of past cruise report cards; unfortunately, there isn't an agreed-upon uniform method of evaluation. Some concerns to monitor as a customer include treatment of bilge water, sewage, and fuel emissions.

THE CRUISE HANDBOOK

SOLO CRUISING

The cruise industry has been changing rapidly as trends in travel shift. That's great news for the increasing number of solo travellers worldwide. Ten years ago, the notion of a cruise catering to the individual was virtually nonexistent. Today many new ships from brands like Cunard Line, Royal Caribbean International, Crystal Cruises, AmaWaterways, Tauck, Viking River Cruises and P&O come equipped with a small supply of studio rooms – often interior cabins – designed with the solo sailor in mind. It's an overdue development after years of charging solo travellers a "single supplement" when they booked a cabin for only themselves, a policy that meant they'd pay a premium of 125% to 175%.

Make sure to shop around when selecting a cruise, as each line has a different policy regarding solo travellers and its solo "tax" can vary. Some travel companies will play matchmaker and link solo cruisers up with one another as roommates to avoid the dreaded supplement charge, while other groups organise specific singles cruises. For megaship travellers, consider hitting up the Cruise Critic community (http://boards. cruisecritic.com) to find other singles signed up for your sailing.

Sociable travellers will have no problem making new connections on small boat tours, especially journeys arranged around common interests, like scuba diving or wine. On large vessels keep an eye out for designated singles mixers on the activities roster, where you can meet and join forces with other solo travellers.

© 2014 MATTEO COLOMBO / GETTY IMAGES

HOW TO AVOID A SOLO SURCHARGE

Try one of these methods to avoid or significantly reduce your undeserved solo penalty

Negotiate
Booking an empty berth on a cruise at the last minute means you probably have some bargaining power. Leverage it to lower the costs of your cabin.

Travel in low season
Sailing during low season will increase the chance that your cruise operator of choice will be willing to waive their solo surcharge in order to fill rooms.

Book with an operator that specialises in singles holidays
Licensed travel agents often are armed with special deals to incentivise their business. They'll be your best advocate for equalising your cruising costs.

Consider sharing a cabin
On smaller and more budget-friendly vessels, berths may be assigned in a more communal fashion. Broadcast your flexibility to the operator to be placed with other solo travellers.

Single and ready to mingle? Try **Singles at Sea** (*www.vacationstogo.com*) or **Singles Cruise** (*www.singlescruise.com*)

© IDREAMPHOTO / SHUTTERSTOCK

Clockwise from top: Indulging in a vacation read on board; snorkeling in Hawaii; sailing the Aegean at sunset

THE CRUISE HANDBOOK

ACCESSIBILITY

When it comes to accessible travel for the differently abled, the cruise industry has some key advantages over land-based travel for tourists needing a wheelchair or vacationers with limited mobility. Any ship that docks at an American port, no matter the flag under which they sail, must comply with the stringent rules laid out by the Americans with Disabilities Act. Cabins may sometimes be smaller than hotel rooms, but staying in one room for the course of a trip smooths out transport issues. Additionally, crew members are trained to assist passengers with accessibility issues during an emergency. Helpful staff can assist at any time while sailing. Assistance for the seeing- and hearing-impaired is readily available as well, including ASL interpreters and closed captioning, and adjustments for the blind include Braille signage and personalised orientations of the vessels. Some large cruise lines operate cruises for vision- and/or hearing-impaired travellers at least once annually.

That said, vessels and ports vary, and due diligence is required. Cruise companies list the accessible features of each boat, and often have a dedicated phone line for special-needs queries. Seek the assistance of one of the 15,000 CLIA-approved agencies to get the lowdown on your ship of choice and guide you to the best options for your needs.

You'll need insider advice on your chosen destinations, like whether or not your cruise ship will be using so-called tender boats to ferry passengers to shore at port. Large cruise ports usually allow cruise ships of all sizes to dock directly, but smaller destinations may require the ship to put anchor at a distance; tenders bridge the gap. Doing so can greatly hamper the ability of mobility-challenged passengers to reach the ports of call, as not all tenders accommodate wheelchairs. Check cruise itineraries carefully and avoid cruises that feature tender destinations, unless they explicitly have special lifts to convey wheelchairs from the cruise ship to the tender, as Holland America does. Keep in mind also that smaller ships may have better luck fitting into ports that are off-limits to megaships.

On board, wheelchairs are provided by the ports for entering and exiting the vessel, but most cruises will expect that you provide your own mobility aid during your time on board. Service animals are given a pass by most large cruises, but emotional support or therapy animals are strictly forbidden. Some cruises are better equipped than others to host passengers with special needs, and it's imperative to seek out the most accessible option before booking. Do your research and you'll have a stress-free trip tailored to your specifications.

THEME CRUISES

Superfans unite! With the plethora of theme cruises on offer, enthusiasts for all types of hobbies and interests can come together and totally geek out touring the seas. Costs tend to be higher with these cruises since the third parties involved keep prices from dropping below the advertised cost, or rack rate, but the added activities and perks more than make up for the price differential. Theme cruises are either full-ship or partial-ship, and may be organised through a charter by an independent company or in a partnership with the cruise line. For example, LGBTQ cruisers might look to operators Atlantis and Olivia.

You may be surprised how many specialised cruises are out there and how diverse their audiences are. Does a nudist cruise strike your fancy? Or maybe you'd rather stay dressed in tennis whites the whole time on a tennis cruise? Cruises exist for every activity and interest imaginable, whether you're a crossword or a Broadway fanatic.

HEALTH & WELLNESS

Around the World Cruises

I mages of indulging in endless platters of coconut shrimp while lounging poolside all day might be the first thing to flash through your mind when thinking about the cruise lifestyle, but taking a cruise can be a fantastic way to change your dietary habits and jumpstart a new exercise regimen. Over the last few years, specifically wellness-focused cruises have proliferated.

It's now possible to sign up for trips filled with yoga workshops, vegan eating, marathon training and Weight Watchers partnerships. There are even cruises to develop your mindfulness or work on overcoming insomnia. Regular cruises, too, have upped the ante with their offerings tailored to general wellbeing. Spaces devoted to state-of-the-art spas and gyms are now as common a fixture on board as the slot machines and dining rooms.

It'll take more than 80 days, but several major cruise lines offer eager travellers the opportunity to circumnavigate the globe. Viking Cruises has a Miami to London (the long way) that takes 128 days; Cunard Line offers a so-called World Voyage in as little as 89 nights.

(See more on pp. 80–85)

WEDDINGS

Give "tying the knot" a nautical twist by getting hitched on the high seas. An easy way to combine the nuptials and honeymoon, cruise weddings offer one-stop shopping for everyone from an eloping couple to a large extended family. The key to a successful cruise wedding is advance planning. The cruise operator or ship's wedding planner can assist with shore versus oboard ceremonies, event spaces, reception details and the legal requirements for a ceremony in your destination of choice.

EATING ON BOARD

Cruises are great for omnivores, but what if you are vegan or gluten-free or have a dietary restriction? Overall awareness of food allergies, sensitivities, religious and ethical eating is on the rise, and tailor-made options on cruises have gone up as a result. Meals for passengers with gluten sensitivity and celiac disease have become commonplace and menus are usually marked. Preparation and communication are the two watchwords to keep in mind: alert the cruise line well in advance of dietary needs or restrictions, and ask staff about how they minimise cross-contamination once on board. Unfortunately,

LiFESAVER TiP

"Try the Indian food in any main dining room on any cruise ship in the world, and it will be some of the best you've ever eaten."

—Mark Tamis,
Royal Caribbean

ships aren't usually nut-free and have varying degrees of safety practices in place, so if a member of your group has a nut allergy (or any other reactivity), make sure to pack your own epinephrine auto-injectors (like EpiPen) as a precaution, even though childcare facilities on major cruise ships keep them on hand. Passengers can give their specific requirements when making their reservation and have staff take it into account throughout the cruise.

There are two routes to take: opt for a megaship with its range of different dining options to satisfy every type of traveller, or choose a small vessel where you can register your specific needs with the culinary crew. You'll be hard-pressed to find a plethora of certified organic menu items on large ships simply due to the cost of the sheer volumes of food needed to sustain a voyage, but small luxury liners oftentimes deliver on this front. Requests for kosher and halal meals can be made with large cruise companies, but if your observance is strict, the best bet for dining kosher is to sign up for a Kosherica voyage (www.kosherica.com).

One thing applies in all cases: if dietary restrictions are a concern, contact your operator of choice before booking your journey to make sure that you'll be satisfied with your potential food selection. Online cruise forums and chat rooms contain a trove of frank discussions about dining options with different operators. Cruise staff are usually well-trained and familiar with all kinds of different dietary demands, and the controlled environment makes it easy to customise meals along your personal preferences. So go ahead, speak up and ask for what you need, because most likely, they'll make it happen.

VEGETARIAN & VEGAN

Not merely a food choice, but a lifestyle, veganism and vegetarianism are sharply on the rise across the globe. Dedicated vegetarian menus are commonplace on luxury vessels with multicourse dining; a chartered all-vegan cruise made history in 2017. Generally speaking, salads have overtaken burgers as the meal of choice on most megaships—going green is trending, vegetarian or not. That said, if you want to avoid second-guessing menu ingredients, try a dedicated vegan cruise like the annual Holistic Holiday at Sea.

CRUISING CALENDAR: WHERE TO GO WHEN

When it comes to planning a cruise, timing can be just as important as the destination. Here's a handy overview of which areas to visit throughout the year.

JANUARY - MARCH

★ This season has the best weather for cruising through the Caribbean, as long as you avoid the crush of families (and higher prices) during March's spring break.
★ Sail through the Panama Canal to take advantage of the short dry season.
★ Winter getting you down? Visit South America in all of its summer glory. Travel down the coast of Peru, Chile or Argentina, and set foot on the continent's most southerly point, Cape Horn.
★ Cooler weather in Southeast Asia makes a great time for river boating in Myanmar or overnighting on a junk in Vietnam's Ha Long Bay.
★ Avoid French Polynesia during these months when the weather can be intensely rainy.
★ The window for travel to Antarctica continues from November and extends through March before the ice pack refreezes.

APRIL - JUNE

★ Book a cruise that stops in Japan in early April (or late March) to witness cherry blossom season.
★ Europe comes into bloom in spring and is the best time to visit aboard a river cruise – especially in Belgium and the Netherlands when the fields of flowers come alive.
★ Consider cruising the Greek Isles in May or June before the onslaught of crowds (both on shore and at sea) overwhelms the region.
★ Spring is a great time to sail the Mediterranean ports in Spain, France and Italy before the summer high season begins.
★ Alaska's shoulder season in May and early June is significantly more cost-effective than trips in high season.

📅 JULY - AUGUST

★ Summer is the best time to go on a transatlantic crossing if you're a sun-worshipper.

★ Scandinavia offers virtually 24 hours of daylight in these months, but if the Northern Lights are on your bucket list, save this trip for midwinter.

★ The Baltic capitals come alive in summer, and on sunny days their crystalline waters can look like the Mediterranean.

★ The rainy monsoon season in Southeast Asia makes trips less ideal during these months.

★ Hurricane season is in full swing in the Caribbean beginning in mid-August, though cheap sailing deals can be found.

📅 SEPTEMBER - OCTOBER

★ Superb weather in Hawaii and Tahiti beckons in early fall, without the summer crowds.

★ Taking in the fall foliage in Canada and New England becomes a must-see obsession from mid-September to mid-October.

★ Cruising season in the Mediterranean simmers down in fall, but the weather is still welcoming and deals can be found during this shoulder season.

★ Consider less traditional cruising destinations like the African coast during these months.

📅 NOVEMBER - DECEMBER

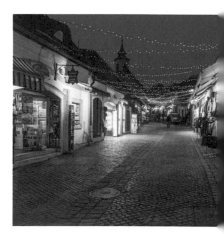

★ Christmas markets explode with holiday cheer in Europe, making river cruising the Danube quite joyous.

★ The short window for seasonal passage to Antarctica starts in November, as the ice pack thaws.

★ South American cruising picks up speed as the weather warms up.

★ The Northern Lights flicker on, perfect for viewing around Iceland, Greenland, the Faroe Islands and other northern destinations.

★ Cyclone season starts the first of November in Australia, but with most storms in March, this is still the most popular time to set sail.

★ Consider a cruise down the Nile River during winter, when temperatures have dropped.

THE CRUISE HANDBOOK

MONEY & BUDGETING

Follow our tried-and-true pointers below for saving money and getting great value. In general, anytime you can arrange an aspect of your trip directly instead of through the cruise line, you'll save.

$ HOW MUCH MONEY DO I REALLY NEED?

Listed prices can seem like they cover everything, until you realise that the cost of transit to the port, drinks on board, and excursions all get added to the picture. Before you book that great-looking rate, make sure to consider beyond the advertised cruise cost of your cabin and meals.

$ HOTEL STAYS

You may want to arrive at your cruise's departure city a day early to reduce the risk of missed connections. Budget for a night's sleep in a hotel or rental accommodation plus two or three meals. Cruise companies have partnerships with local lodging, though it can be more cost efficient to square that away on your own if you don't mind the extra legwork.

$ TRANSIT

Unless you have a port in your own city, you'll have to fly to embark on the cruise of your dreams. Check that airfares are reasonable for the dates you are considering before getting swept away in a cruise bargain. Then, don't forget to factor in the costs of on-the-ground transportation. That includes transfers to and from your hometown airport and the costs of reaching the pier from your arrival airport. Cruise lines can take care of your transfer costs at a premium; it's also possible to arrange your own taxi or rideshare or even to take public transit. Just triple check your departure and arrival times so you don't miss the boat.

$ FOOD & BEVERAGE

One of the trademark elements of cruising is the all-inclusive dining, but that doesn't mean everything's included in your booking. On many megaships, for example, you'll find a bevy of specialty dining options which are not incorporated in your base fare, and must be paid for à la carte. Decide beforehand if you are willing to pay extra for certain meals, so that you can realistically estimate your additional costs. On a budget but still want to celebrate? Select the number of specialty meals you're OK with spending money on – and stick to it. Taking a look at your own budget and how you want to allocate your money in advance will keep you from making impulse decisions whose price tag you'll regret afterwards.

Alcohol, soft drinks and designer coffees come at an extra cost too, and one that can really add up if you make a habit of them. On traditional cruising vessels you'll be able to purchase beverage packages on your first day aboard, or you can ask beforehand if there are discounts for purchasing packages in advance. Lastly, while all-you-can-drink deals are easily attainable, take the extra ten minutes to do some simple math and make sure the inclusive drink offerings actually make sense for you. Ask yourself how many alcoholic beverages, soft drinks and coffees you have consumed in the last week – and then assume you'll drink more than that when on your vacation. Generally on holiday, we consume more food and beverage than we do in our everyday lives, so accounting for double your at-home consumption should suffice. If you're not going to consume around 35 alcoholic beverages during a weeklong voyage, a drinks package is probably not for you.

$ EXCURSIONS

On adventure cruises and expedition-like vessels, the excursions are the major draw, with at least some included in your quoted rate. On classic cruising itineraries like in the Caribbean and Mediterranean, onshore activities come at an extra cost. For recreational excursions like scuba diving, windsurfing or snowshoeing, you'll need to book through the cruise line or research independent tour providers in advance. Take a look at the ship's itinerary in advance and decide which experiences are a priority for you.

Planning to take in the city sights or go to the beach? Try exploring on your own via public transportation and Google Maps. It's a great way to experience a port of call – so long as you pay careful attention to when you need to be back on the ship.

THE CRUISE HANDBOOK

$ OFTEN OVER-LOOKED COSTS

There are certain costs to travel that often run under the radar. The most obvious way to reduce costs is to take a budget cruise alternative instead of hopping on a megaship (like a houseboat in Kerala, India or a Blue Cruise in Turkey), or steer clear of casinos unless you have a strict limit on what you're OK with spending (and losing). However, the smaller, easily-forgotten purchases, charges and fees can add up. So consider these ancillary costs ahead of time to avoid being blindsided. A little planning ahead will help on all fronts.

Below: Blue cruises on Turkey's Turquoise Coast are prime targets for asking about BYOB

$ SOUVENIR SHOPPING

When it comes to souvenir shopping, setting a budget with your spending is crucial. Try allotting yourself one special purchase as a memento of your trip. Do your shopping away from the strip of real estate right by the port, where tourist traps proliferate. Onboard shopping can be just as dangerous for the wallet, with megaships designed to get you to spend on photo opportunities and other pricey buys. If you're travelling as a family, communicate what purchases will be made for children in advance, before you're stuck saying "no" in a gift shop and facing a possible tantrum.

$ ATM FEES

Onboard currency exchangers and port-side ATMs come with hefty fees. Apply in advance for a credit card with no foreign transaction fees for the spending you do off ship, but also remember that not everyone will take a credit card. You can change your money into the local currency before you depart.

$ INTERNET ACCESS

Most ships have internet access, some with relatively high-speed connectivity, but internet fees at sea are quite expensive, ranging from around US$0.35 per MB (about three minutes of Facebook time) to US$25 per day of wi-fi usage. Forego this to add instant savings to your trip and get a digital detox, or find a workaround to remain partially connected. Get in touch with your mobile phone service operator before you leave and consider purchasing a limited roaming plan. In port you'll be able to access the local destination's cellular service, which can significantly save on connectivity costs. Lastly, turn your phone to "airplane mode" when you're at sea to ensure that your phone isn't racking up auxiliary roaming charges.

15 ADDITIONAL TIPS FOR SAVING MONEY

1. Surf the deals in "wave season." Wave season is industry lingo for the period from January to March when the bulk of bookings are made. To lure in vacationers planning their yearly getaways, cruise lines offer upgrades, onboard credit or even 50% off a second fare.

2. Travel in the off-season. Sailing in low season means big discounts on classic cruising destinations like Alaska and the Caribbean.

3. Capitalise on last-minute deals. When cruises can't fill their cabins they drastically drop their prices at the last minute to find passengers. Budget travellers in Ushuaia, Argentina often wait around for day-of discounted voyages to Antarctica – the same applies for any cruise if you're willing to be spontaneous.

4. Book your next trip on board. Enjoying your first cruise? Book your next passage before disembarking and you'll reap the benefits of loyalty rewards and automatic cabin upgrades.

5. Leverage your discounts. A plethora of discounts in all shapes and sizes are available, as long as you ask. Your cruise may offer price knockdowns for army veterans, senior citizens, students and more.

6. Take a "Repositioning" cruise. When ships move between cruise regions in response to seasonal trends, say from the Mediterranean and the Caribbean as summer ends, cabins are made available to help defray the costs of repositioning the vessel. Oftentimes these one-way itineraries have many "at-sea" days, but the onboard amenities remain the same at a fraction of the price.

7. Bundle your fare. That too-good-to-be-true cruise fare can come with hidden costs, namely the transportation fees from your home to the ship's point of departure. Seek bundled fares that combine the cruise cost with airfare (and sometimes onshore excursions).

8. Get a cabin guarantee. Rather than pick a specific cabin, you can lock into a room-type tier on a large cruise, guaranteeing a minimum level of comfort. If your chosen category fills up, you're automatically bumped up to the next level without paying the difference.

9. Call a partner agent. Most cruising companies work with licensed agents. They have the power to provide you with extra incentives and deals, so it's worth scouting one out.

10. Sign up for email blasts. If you have a destination or cruise line of choice, it's worth signing up for regular emails to be the first in the know about discounts and news. General vacationing sites like Travelzoo (www.travelzoo.com) can keep you up-to-date on deals as well.

11. Sail on older vessels. All that's shiny and new commands a higher dollar value. Freshly minted vessels regularly charge more, so opt for a craft that's a couple of years old – the buzz dwindles but the modern conveniences will be similar.

12. Engage on social media. Following cruise lines on Twitter, Facebook or Instagram is another handy way of scouting deals and discounts. Keep an eye out for giveaways, too.

13. Ask for money back. If fares lower after you book, don't despair. If you're paying via installments, you can ask the operator to reduce your last payment to take advantage of the new discounted pricing. Already paid in full? Contact the cruise line and see if you can get onboard credit in compensation.

14. Pick interior cabins. Let's be honest, you're not taking a trip to lock yourself away in your cabin all day, so consider a windowless room. Some vessels also have "promenade" rooms with windows looking out onto an interior space.

15. Ask about BYOB. On smaller vessels it doesn't hurt to ask if you can bring your own drinks on board. You'll toast the savings.

BOOKING YOUR TRIP

You've done your research and figured out which ship and destination are the right match for you. Now it's time to book your trip! Here are a few additional things to consider.

$ DIRECT BOOKING VS TRAVEL AGENT

Even for the most seasoned globe-trotter used to handling all their own accommodations, it can be useful to work with a travel agent when booking your cruise. CLIA offers special accreditation to agents, most of whom have firsthand experience with the cruises they book. Speed date with a couple of agents and tell them exactly what you're after.

Capable cruise consultants should be able to isolate the best trip option for you after a few minutes discussing your preferences on the phone. They also have incentivised access to extra perks and upgrades for their clients – don't be afraid to ask about those, too. With no extra cost to you for working with an agent, it's a no-brainer.

$ WHICH CABIN DO I PICK?

On river cruises and small ships, most cabins are the same shape and size. If you're worried about being seasick, request a room on a lower deck as close to the middle of the ship as possible. Megaships have dozens of different cabin types from interior rooms to suites with balconies. Think critically about how your itinerary is shaping up – if you're going to be out on shore excursions all day every day, then it's hardly worth having a balcony. If you're claustrophobic or cringe at the thought of not having natural light, then it's worth avoiding an interior cabin. It's worth having a look at the floor plan of your vessel of choice to orient yourself with the ship's design, and then decide how close or how far removed you want to be from the public spaces.

If pricing is your biggest factor in cabin selection, be strategic with timing. Bookings done eight months or more before departure generally yield the highest value; last-minute bookings (two weeks before departure) can also be advantageous when ships are trying to fill cabins.

$ RAINY-DAY WOES

Sure, the terminology varies across the globe – hurricane, cyclone, monsoon – but they all mean the same thing: rain. An ideal cruise trip involves negotiating the water below, not having it bucket down on you from above, so research seasonal rain patterns before booking. Not all storm seasons are created equal. Average weather statistics are easily searchable online, and it's worth digging into your destination of choice – you may find, for example, that certain Caribbean Islands like the Grenadines and Aruba aren't even located along the region's notorious hurricane belt, making them worthy options in the off-season.

SELECTING INSURANCE

"Whether you're cruising on an ocean liner, smaller riverboat or chartering your own vessel, your insurance travel plan should have comprehensive medical up to US$50,000 and emergency transportation benefits up to US$1 million, as travelling over international waters means potentially being hours or days away from a port of call with high-quality, intensive care facilities. Also, more adventurous cruisers need to read their policies for any limitations or exclusions – oftentimes riskier water sports (like scuba diving below 120 feet or without a divemaster) are not included in their coverage." – *Matt Popowski, External Communications Specialist, Allianz Global Assistance USA (www. allianztravelinsurance.com)*

CRUISE PLANNING TIMELINE

1 YEAR BEFORE Dream. Think about where you want to go and start collecting information about the voyage and destination. Get inspired by magazines, guidebooks and websites.

9 MONTHS BEFORE Consider booking your cabin now. It might sound early but if you're planning on travelling in high season, know that popular passages often fill up a full year in advance.

6 MONTHS BEFORE Finalise your travel dates around your cruise of choice, ask for appropriate time off from work, set flight tracker alerts for discount airfare, and make sure your travel documents and vaccinations are up to date.

4 MONTHS BEFORE Book your flights and your pre- and post-cruise accommodations. Purchase your travel insurance, and start researching excursion possibilities more intensely.

2 MONTHS BEFORE Arrange your shore excursions, rental vehicles, restaurant bookings, airport and port transfers, and start booking onboard items like premium dining and spa treatments.

1 MONTH BEFORE Use social media to broadcast your upcoming trip – who knows, you might have a friend visiting your destination of choice at the same time as you. If you are paying for your trip in installments, your last payment will likely be due.

1 WEEK (OR LESS) BEFORE Organise all the items you wish to pack, making sure your electronics are appropriately charged. Sort any medication refills. Make sure your luggage is tagged. Contact your mobile phone carrier about international calling, visit your bank to acquire foreign currency and notify them about potential unusual spending.

PLANNING YOUR OWN CHARTER

Looking for the seafaring lifestyle that a ship affords but want the autonomy of a tailor-made itinerary? Ian Pedersen, sailing expert and product manager of The Moorings (www.moorings.com), weighs in on the most important tips and tricks to organising the perfect charter cruising experience.

WHAT DO YOU NEED TO KNOW BEFORE ORGANISING YOUR OWN CHARTER?

Charter vacations primarily take place on sailing yachts, however, there are also power catamarans available to more experienced boaters. For any trip you should know the basics of boating: tying lines and fenders, anchoring, picking up a mooring ball and understanding navigational markers. If you don't know "port" from "starboard," consider hiring a captain or opt for an all-inclusive, crewed boat.

HOW DO YOU HIRE A CREW?

Generally speaking, crewed charters for vacations consist of a captain and a chef. Oftentimes they're a couple that live on a yacht full-time. There are thousands of private, individually-owned, crewed yachts out there, and many companies – like The Moorings – offer a clear and reliable standard of service around the world. Most of these charters are all-inclusive, and cover your food and beverage for your time on board. If you want more flexibility, like carving out opportunities to eat and play offshore, consider hiring just a captain instead.

WHAT SKILLS DO YOU NEED FOR A SOLO TRIP?

You should be comfortable captaining boats over 30 feet in length, and will be required to show proof of prior experience before confirming your reservation. The Caribbean is generally more relaxed about required skills, however, in the Mediterranean you'll need a formal International Certification to hire a charter.

WHAT SHOULD YOU PACK?

Pack as little as possible. Here are the essentials: a bathing suit, sunglasses, a good hat, lots of sunscreen and your favorite playlist. Living on a yacht is a lot less glamorous and luxurious than it sounds. Embrace existing almost exclusively in your bathing suit and tying your wet clothes to the deck to let the sea air-dry them out. Leave your beauty accessories at home and enjoy the "boat hair, don't care" attitude. Don't forget a pair of flip-flops (thongs) or sandals, and one pair of closed-toe shoes for onshore activities.

WHAT ARE SOME COMMON MISCONCEPTIONS ABOUT CHARTERING?

A charter is not a cruise – it is not a predetermined vacation with a set itinerary, nor are you travelling on the same vessel with hundreds of strangers. You are free to go wherever you wish, but generally, charter vacations aren't ocean-faring – they're offered in regions where you only sail an hour or two at a time to get from one place to the next with the aim of going ashore to explore.

See p. 77 for some intel on the best places in the world to hire a charter vessel.

DiY CRUiSiNG

If you've dreamed of dropping everything to spend an extended period of time at sea, a DIY cruise might be just the thing. Here, the Johnson family of Elcie Expeditions lay out all of the essential need-to-knows about seeing the world via your own watercraft.

Richard Johnson, Jessica Rice Johnson, both originally from Maryland, and their two teenage daughters, Emma and Molly, live aboard Elcie (www.elcieexpeditions.com), a 62-foot New Zealand-built catamaran currently completing a full circumnavigation of the globe.

HOW DiD YOU DECiDE TO PURCHASE YOUR OWN VESSEL?

Having worked on boats for other organisations, we were always confined to their schedules. I recall sailing within a quarter mile of an island, seeing an inviting waterfront and not being able to stop because it wasn't on the itinerary. We were looking for freedom with our travel plans, and a boat was the perfect way to travel because you essentially take your house with you.

Elcie is a result of many years of sailing on different vessels, bringing together all of the ideal qualities we wanted in a long-distance cruising sailboat: strength, large water and diesel storage capacity, a shallow draft, extra accommodation space to help earn an income, and a craft that's gentle on the environment.

WHAT ARE THE KEY ELEMENTS TO MAKING A DiY ADVENTURE HAPPEN?

Pre-Budgeting

For under US$100,000 you can purchase a boat that needs work, or a modest yet very capable cruiser. Many people pick up work along the way to help with cruising costs, like internet-based jobs or local mechanical repairs. It's possible to find seasonal work ashore in some countries if you are eligible through a work visa or can be paid in cash under the table. The biggest expense to factor in is the insurance – it's the highest ticket item after the equipment. We have an especially large liability coverage because we carry passengers – you can get away with spending less if it's just a couple or family on board.

Deciding to Buy or Build

The advantage of building your own boat is the sweat equity from designing a vessel that specifically suits your needs – but we would definitely not recommend this path for someone who is new to the industry. It took us three long years to build Elcie in a professional shipbuilding yard – we'd spend weekends laboring away while watching other boats heading out for a sail.

Training

It's a steep learning curve, so do everything you can to increase your knowledge: take classes in diesel mechanics, navigation, safety and first aid. Try crewing on other boats first, and for your first time doing an offshore passage, join a rally, where multiple boats all travel together. There's comfort in numbers and having a support network around you before trying long hauls on your own. The ARC Rally (www.worldcruising.com/arc/event.aspx) is a good example of an organised mass migration with safety checks, radio networks and assistance clearing customs. (Both Richard and Jessica have a 200 Ton USCG License valid in all waters of the world.)

THE CRUISE HANDBOOK

Cruising Expenses

Expenses will vary depending on where you cruise and what your comfort requires. The Panama Canal, for example, is extremely expensive to get through. The Galapagos, Easter Island and French Polynesia also rank as some of the most expensive areas to cruise. On the other hand, Fiji and Indonesia are much more budget friendly. Other things that will affect your cruising budget are your meal plans (are you happy eating fish and rice or do you want to eat in fancy restaurants when you land?), your onshore expenses like renting a car, docking versus anchoring, and how fast you travel/how much fuel you burn.

TELL US ABOUT YOUR FIRST CIRCUMNAVIGATION.

Originally, we set out with the idea of doing an 18-month circumnavigation, however we were having so much fun and realised how much there was to see that our trip around the world lasted nearly four years: 1997 to 2001. Like we do now, we also invited expense-sharing crew to join along. We didn't have the internet as a marketing tool back then, so we relied on magazine ads to advertise and snail mail to communicate with potential crew. Word of mouth brought us many crew members – friends of friends who had sailed with us before. Back then we used to send a page-long fax to family once a month; now we're almost always in constant contact. I'm still not sure which one I prefer!

On that journey, sailing in the Middle East and up the Red Sea was a highlight, with stops in Oman, Yemen, Eritrea, Sudan, Egypt and Israel. The diving was spectacular and the landscape otherworldly. It is, however, an area that's far less safe now because of piracy and anti-American sentiments.

When we started off, I thought it was important

"There's something to be said for being able to cook in your own kitchen and sleep in your own bed every night while always changing location."

to have the route and all the details determined in advance – I soon realised that plans quickly change, especially when you learn about an intriguing island or a new port to visit. That's how we ended up sleeping on the floor of a Dayak village chief's house way up in the hills of interior Kalimantan.

WHAT WERE THE MOST UNEXPECTED OBSTACLES YOU'VE HAD ON YOUR JOURNEY?

Maintaining three things: our finances, our home and our sanity. There's a joke that the meaning of BOAT is Break Out Another Thousand – marine equipment can be very expensive. While many people sell everything to be unencumbered and have more cash in their cruising kitty, we have kept our house so that we can spend time there when not abroad. It's been difficult keeping a house while we're out sailing, but it gives our girls an anchor and sense of place to counterbalance our nomadic lifestyle. Plus the work to get our boat completed forced us to find fortitude and patience before we could start sailing.

ANY INSIGHT INTO RENTING A VESSEL INSTEAD OF BUYING?

I would recommend "bareboating" (captaining your own vessel) before taking the plunge. All of the most popular cruising grounds will have bareboating charter options, like the Caribbean, Greece and Tahiti. It's an affordable way to test the waters, so

- New Zealand
- Fiji
- French Polynesia
- Pitcairn Island
- Indonesia

**Above: Richard Johnson,
Jessica Rice Johnson and
their two teenage daughters
on their circumnavigaton**

to speak, and see if long-distance cruising is truly for you. But bear in mind that on a charter you are likely confined to protected waters and are required to be anchored before sunset.

Offshore passages are very different – contrary winds, seasickness and long night watches result in cranky crews. Try a website that offers matchmaking for crews and skippers – Tinder for boats – like FindACrew (www.findacrew.net), CrewSeekers (www.crewseekers.net) and Offshore Passage Opportunities (www.sailopo.com). For more intensive offshore training, there are programs like Mahina Expeditions (www.mahina.com) and Skip Novak's Pelagic (www.pelagic.co.uk).

HOW DOES SOMEONE BECOME A PASSENGER ON THE ELCIE?

People join us to gain offshore sailing experience and multi-haul experience, to tick something off of their bucket list, or simply to have some holiday adventure. We have an application process (that can be filled out online) with questions regarding prior sailing and travel experience to help vet potential travellers, but find that it's somewhat self-selecting, attracting people who are interested in the notion of sailing with no land in sight. All who join us are considered to be a part of the crew – we don't call them passengers. Expense-sharing crew come along for a segment of our predetermined schedule. A leg may last anywhere from six to thirty-one days depending on the distance we need to cover. We've designed the journey around places of interest and major airports to facilitate some travel ease. While the new crew shares in the ship's responsibilities, including the night watch, there's plenty of time for offshore exploration.

Visit the Elcie website (www.elcieexpeditions.com) for more information about their epic circumnavigation.

THE CRUISE HANDBOOK

TOP 10 REASONS TO CRUISE

1 CONVENIENCE

Time is often the biggest limiting factor for travel. You only get a handful of vacation days, and you want to maximise your adventure. A cruise can be a clever way to tick a few destination boxes on your bucket list by enjoying the abridged version of each day's port stop as you tour its highlights. The bonus? You don't need to pack and unpack each night.

2 STRESS-FREE PLANNING

Planning a holiday while balancing a demanding job or at-home responsibilities can make taking a vacation feel more like a chore than a relief. Have no fear. With a cruise, an entire package – flights, cabin and food – can be booked with the click of a single button, and you can figure out the nitty-gritty activities and excursions when you get on board and finally have a chance to exhale.

3 VALUE

"All-inclusive" is the key word of the cruising industry and it can be a boon for the budget, especially in the family travel category. Dining options on large ships are expansive, as are playtime opportunities for the kids. Even the entertainment on larger vessels has become Broadway caliber and is already included in your booking price.

4 LUXURY

At the other end of the spectrum, cruises today comprise some of the most ambitious additions to the luxury travel market, from private barges that elegantly swish along the waters of provincial France to upmarket cruisers of hotel-esque proportions sporting submarine excursions, private plunge pools and world-class art collections.

5 PURSUE YOUR PASSION ON BOARD

Themed cruises, or journeys with a particular educational focus, can be the perfect way to delve deeper into a subject of interest – from archaeology and art history to photography or marine biology – with lectures offered by specialists and scientists. It's also a great way to meet like-minded people and forge new friendships.

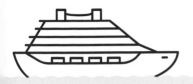

6 FOOD FEASTS

No, we're not talking about the all-you-can-eat ribs served at midnight. Much like the way Las Vegas has become a test kitchen for international food artists, cruises are striving for greatness by engaging acclaimed chefs in fine-dining restaurant partnerships and offering cooking classes for passengers.

7 EXPLORATION

Be your own Captain Picard! Cruises go where no one has gone before (or very few people, at least). Travelling by boat affords you the opportunity to see the roadless recesses of Alaska in the midnight sun's glow, visit otherwise inaccessible jungle-fringed Polynesian islands, meet highland tribesmen in upriver Papua New Guinea, or follow in Shackleton's footsteps on Antarctica.

8 CONNECT WITH NATURE

Safaris are no longer relegated to vehicular exploration. In fact, small boats do just as admirable a job of getting close to nature. Spot exotic birds and lizards in the Galapagos, kayak between breaching whales in the northern and southern seas, spot polar bears in Svalbard, sight the sea lions in Australia, dip underwater to scuba dive with sharks and stingrays or sail beside roving elephants in Africa's interior.

9 WELLNESS

You may associate cruises with overeating and binge drinking, but most cruise lines have been responding in kind to the spiking interest in health and wellbeing. Expansive spas, monstrous gyms, sports classes and clean eating options are readily available on virtually all megaships. Smaller sailings afford passengers the opportunity to slow their heart rates down and practice some self-led meditation.

10 DIGITAL DETOX

Though the phrase "digital detox" has become a bit of a cliché, there's something to be said for looking up from your smartphone and seeing the world around you. It's easy to unplug on a cruise, whether because the internet connectivity can be prohibitively expensive or because you're sailing through a remote part of the globe sans cellular service. Enjoy it while it lasts, before the whole world has wi-fi.

⚓ CRUISE YOUR WAY QUIZ

Not sure where to start with your planning? Take our cruise quiz to figure out the type of trip that's right for you.

1. WHAT'S YOUR BIGGEST CRUISING FEAR?

a) That we'll have bad weather

b) That I'll be bored on board

c) That I won't get enough time to experience the destinations I'm visiting

d) That I'll be surrounded by too many strangers

2. WHICH OF THE FOLLOWING DESTINATIONS IS AT THE TOP OF YOUR TRAVEL TO-DO LIST?

a) Jamaica

b) The Galapagos

c) France

d) Moorea

3. WHAT IS THE BEST REASON TO TRAVEL BY SHIP OR BOAT?

a) Taking a break from the real world

b) Visiting places unreachable by car

c) Experiencing destinations without any unpacking

d) New frontiers for adventure

4. WHO IS YOUR FAVORITE TRAVEL COMPANION?

a) My kids

b) My spouse

c) My friends

d) Myself

5. WHAT'S YOUR FAVOURITE FOOD?

a) Cheeseburger—a classic!

b) A big salad

c) Sushi

d) Freshly made ceviche

6. HOW DO YOU PACK FOR A HOLIDAY?

a) I pack everything I own

b) I wish I was more minimal, but always overpack

c) I leave room to buy new things when I'm abroad

d) Two of everything and call it a day

7. YOU'RE TAKING A WEEKLONG STAYCATION. WHAT DO YOU DO?

a) Catch up on missed TV

b) Clean eating and a new exercise regime

c) Museums, restaurants, and wine bars. Lather, rinse, repeat

d) Explore the unknown corners of my hometown

8. YOU GET $1000 AS A GIFT, WHAT DO YOU USE IT FOR?

a) A weekend getaway at a fancy hotel

b) A new camera

c) An ultra-lavish meal out on the town

d) A plane ticket

9. WHAT KIND OF SOUVENIR ARE YOU LIKELY TO BRING HOME FROM A TRIP?

a) Jewelry

b) Photos

c) Cheese, liquor and/or spices

d) I take only memories and leave only footprints

10. YOUR TRAVEL PARTNER ISN'T KEEN TO VISIT A LOCAL SITE, SO YOU:

a) Get over it; stay with your pal

b) Convince your plus-one to have a little look-see

c) Quickly check it out solo, then join back up

d) Head off on your own

11. I NEVER LEAVE HOME WITHOUT:

a) My phone

b) A credit card

c) A snack

d) A smile

12. WHAT KIND OF CAMERA DO YOU BRING ON YOUR TRAVELS?

a) My smartphone's good enough!

b) An SLR camera and an extra lens for the landscapes

c) A small, high-quality clicker, so I don't look like a total tourist

d) The latest GoPro

13. YOU'RE HOSTING A DINNER PARTY, WHAT'S ON THE MENU?

a) I order take-out!

b) Anything that can be cooked on the barbecue

c) A new recipe for *laksa*

d) Home-cured charcuterie

14. PICK YOUR FAVOURITE OCEAN MOVIE FROM THOSE BELOW:

a) *Titanic*

b) *Master and Commander*

c) *Pirates of the Caribbean*

d) *Cast Away*

15. IN AN EMERGENCY, YOU'RE THE PERSON WHO TENDS TO:

a) Let someone else take care of it

b) Lend a helping hand

c) Recruit the right person to pitch in

d) Pull an Olivia Pope— it's handled!

16. WHAT'S YOUR FAVOURITE ANIMAL?

a) A sloth

b) A snow leopard

c) A horse

d) A shark

17. WHAT'S YOUR IDEA OF AN ADRENALINE RUSH?

a) Riding an escalator

b) Going down a water slide

c) A night in a haunted house

d) Scuba diving

18. DESCRIBE THE PERFECT SATURDAY NIGHT:

a) Netflix and pizza delivery

b) Cottage at the lake

c) Drinks out with friends

d) Trying the newest restaurant in town

19. HOW DO YOU FEEL ABOUT MOVIE SPOILERS?

a) I like to know the ending before I watch it

b) Plot twists are great, but I don't like big surprises

c) Film is about the characters

d) I don't even want to know what it's about before I see it!

20. WHAT KIND OF CULTURE SHOCK EXCITES YOU?

a) There's nothing exciting about culture shock

b) Visiting a small village surrounded by stunning nature

c) Language immersion

d) Feeling like I'm the first to discover a destination

RESULTS

≫——→

THIS WAY

THE CRUISE HANDBOOK

RESULTS

MOSTLY As - Relax on a megaship with all the bells and whistles It's not so much about the destination – you're looking to relax and unwind. And so you should! You've been slaving away at work, and vacations are a way to unplug. Lucky for you, megaships now come complete with every indulgence and distraction imaginable, including delicious dining. You can breeze through the Caribbean without ever having to disembark in a port because you'll find everything on board, from Broadway-level musicals to Escape the Room experiences and a luxe spa.

MOSTLY Bs - Explore new frontiers on an adventure cruise You're looking for a cruise journey where you can take in some of the world's most beautiful vistas. A classic Alaskan cruise might be a great place to start, or kick things up a notch and explore the barren recesses of Patagonia, Antarctica or even Svalbard, especially if the possibility of spotting whales or rare birds excites you just as much as capturing that perfect sunset Insta. You're ready to embrace nature's majesty, but want a soft pillow on which to rest your head at the end of the day.

MOSTLY Cs - Enjoy the local vibe on a small ship or river cruise You're a total culture vulture, making a small vessel the right fit for you. One of Europe's river cruises could be the perfect match for you, spending your days in small villages, perhaps at Christmas time exploring the festive seasonal markets. Or maybe visiting the interior tribesmen of Papua New Guinea piques your interest. Either way, it's about the people and the culture that make up the fabric of a destination, and a cruise journey is your ideal way to take it all in.

MOSTLY Ds - Immerse yourself in a region aboard a small boat or self-charter Adventure is your middle name, and boat travel is just another way to peel back the layers of a new destination. You want to keep things intimate with your own chartered craft or liveaboard a small vessel with only a handful of other passengers. Maybe scuba diving becomes the centerpiece of your trip, or it's about learning the ropes of sailing and alighting on far-flung tropical islets. You're looking for something unconventional, authentic and highly personalised.

PLANNING

TOP 10 PLANNING TIPS

1 KNOW WHICH CRUISE TYPE IS RIGHT FOR YOU

So you've decided that your next trip is going to be on a cruise – great! Now you have to figure out which type of journey is the right one for you. This is not a decision you should take lightly; the cruising world has every type of experience imaginable from 6000-passenger megaships to teeny, self-chartered sailboats. If you haven't already, take the quiz on p. 44 to discover your best cruise type.

2 ACQUAINT YOURSELF WITH THE DIFFERENT CRUISE LINES

In the same way you make conscious shopping decisions when purchasing lifestyle items like clothing and food, cruise selection should involve some due-diligence research. Some megaships cater to families, others promise more of a party and smaller vessels target a specific market. Sure, your main goal may not be making new friends on board, but carefully consider which line feels like the best fit.

3 CONSIDER A TRAVEL AGENT

Sounds pretty retro, doesn't it? But cruise travel isn't like other trips, in that once you're underway, you can't troubleshoot and recalibrate. An agent acts as your eyes and ears, scouting different vessels before you venture on board. First-time cruisers should use agents to get a clearer sense of which cruise size, brand, and destination is the best fit for them.

4 THINK BEYOND THE TRADITIONAL CRUISE

Going on a cruise doesn't have to mean massive salad bars and midnight conga lines. We live in a brave new world of boating that includes travel by science vessel or cargo ship – you can even rent your own vessel on Airbnb! Theme cruises, as well, come in all sorts of shapes and sizes from EDM trance-a-thons to intensive cooking academies at sea. If you can think it up, then it probably already exists. Dream big.

5 START EARLY

If you're a planner and don't expect to jump on last-minute discount deals, then plan well in advance, especially if you're keen to travel during high season. Check out the booking timeline on p. 35 to learn how to optimise your cruising experience by getting the ball rolling in the months before you travel.

6 YOU DON'T NEED THE FANCIEST CABIN

Unless you're planning on doing a transatlantic voyage and spending a week staring out at the open sea, you probably don't need to have the most luxe quarters on the ship. Even on at-sea days, there are plenty of common spaces (both indoors and outdoors) for hanging out. Think of it like picking the smallest house on the nicest block; opt for tighter digs on an upgraded ship instead of splashing out on an older vessel.

7 BOOK YOUR OWN OFF-SHIP EXCURSIONS

It's worth planning in advance to get the most out of each port stop. If you're opting for a DIY experience on land, take time before your trip to familiarise yourself with distances from the port to your desired attractions. This will help avoid taxi gouging at the pier, and ensure that you're back at the ship well before it departs. It also doesn't hurt to recruit new friends once on board to help defray touring costs.

8 THINK ABOUT SUSTAINABILITY

It's important to be thinking globally about your footprint when traveling, especially in remote corners of the globe. Ask your cruise about onboard initiatives to reduce waste and promote recycling. Look into the social sustainability of your cruise as well – is your boat supporting the local economies of the destinations it visits? Some ships even offer shoreside voluntourism opportunities.

9 DON'T SUCCUMB TO SEASICKNESS

Even the best-laid cruising plans can be ruined by nausea. If you're prone to motion sickness, choose a cruise that makes inner passages only instead of spending extended amounts of time on the open sea (like transatlantic crossings, repositioning voyages and polar journeys). Come prepared with your seasickness remedy of choice and choose a room in the middle of the ship on a lower level.

10 EXTEND YOUR TRIP

Consider adding a few days before or after your cruise to explore on land. Especially if you're embarking from a city or country that's new to you, extra time around your cruise itinerary will deepen your experience of the region. This can be done as a cruisetour or be self-booked.

THE CRUISE HANDBOOK

STAYING HEALTHY ON BOARD

Seasickness prevention
For those cursed with bouts of wave-induced nausea, consider the following tips and tricks from Dr. Benjamin Shore, the chief medical consultant at Royal Caribbean Cruises, to keep your belly at ease.

● **Seasickness tablets**
Meclizine (Bonine) and Dramamine are two popular preventative pills for mal de mer. Beware though: when mixed with alcohol, travellers can experience intense drowsiness.
Dr. Shore: "Meclizine is an effective antihistamine seasickness medication, but it has the common side effect of sedation, and a long list of medical contraindications related to its antihistamine effect."

● **The 'patch' (transdermal cinnarizine or scopolomine)**
Eight to twelve hours before a journey on rough seas, place this sticky patch on your neck beneath your ear to help alleviate seasickness.
Dr. Shore: "The patch is quite effective for three days at each application. It does, however, have common side effects such as dry mouth and sedation, and

some uncommon but serious side effects such as agitation and confusion. Travellers must handle the patch carefully so as to not touch one's eye and cause dilated pupils. It is best applied prior to the onset of symptoms; it is not effective otherwise."

● **Natural remedies**
Ginger can be consumed in tea, candy, or pill form and is a common palliative for calming motion sickness. Some cruisers find that eating dry crackers or chomping on green apples helps abate their symptoms. Others find that smelling certain aromas does the trick.

Dr. Shore: "Anecdotally, ginger seems to be helpful, and some people find various aromas helpful as well. Dry crackers seem to help a bit after the onset of seasickness. An odd but easy solution seems to be the smelling of newspaper print. I don't know why this effect works so well, but it actually seems to diminish the sensation of nausea."

● **Acupressure wristbands**
A fabric band with a small, stitched-in plastic bead that presses on the soft, veiny portion of the wrist at the Nei-Kuan acupressure point is another tactic. The Sea-Band is one example of several. Borrowed from Chinese medicine, the act of applying pressure to this specific point on the wrists is thought to lessen stomach pain and nausea.

● **Mindfulness and meditation**
Some claim that meditation and mindfulness can pull one out of motion sickness, especially doing it above deck with deep breathing, noticing the natural world around them, repeating a mantra, or doing some activity. With this in mind, it may be more about the actions taken and paired with prayer and meditation that are the remedy. All the more reason to get out above deck when you're seasick.

● **Factors on ship**
If you know that you're prone to seasickness, don't sign up for a cruise that tackles a significant amount of open water. Opt instead for inside passages or river cruises. If you do take an open-water passage, larger ships will be more stable. Try to book a cabin in the middle of the ship on a lower floor to minimise the rocking motion in your quarters. Should seasickness set in, while it may seem counterintuitive, hibernating in your cabin can lead to more nausea. Head to a breezy deck area to cool down your core body temperature. Breathing in fresh air and watching the horizon can reduce malaise.

PACKING PRACTICALITIES

O ne of the biggest perks of cruise travel is not having to be a packing savant. Once you're on board you won't need to live out of your suitcase. You can keep it in your room however you like, or better yet, put it all away in your cabin's closets and drawers. Follow the advice below and you'll be ready to roll.

suitcase with versions of your own. These guidelines have been drafted with the wisdom of a thousand crossings and will give you crucial information needed for packing right.

NO FANCY BAGS NEEDED

Thinking about splurging on that fancy bag at REI with all the hidden zippers, trapdoors and a surplus of storage compartments? Don't buy it. You don't need a suitcase that earns its sticker shock with engineered ergonomics – you'll be unpacking it as soon as you get on board.

CHECK THE CRUISE'S WEBSITE

Before you fold even one sock to pack in your suitcase, go straight to your cruise's website and carefully read their suggested packing list. If your arctic adventure operator tells you that waterproof boots and lined windbreakers will be provided, do not waste precious space in your

BRING A TOTE OR DRAWSTRING BACKPACK

It sounds almost too simple, but you'll want something lightweight that isn't a purse or a carry-on backpack to lug around your belongings (like sunscreen, camera, beach reading etc.) whether it's off the ship or over to another part of the vessel. You don't want to

get stuck having to overpay for a schlocky souvenir sack.

GO FORMAL

You may have heard this before: if you look the part, you might get the role. For men, consider bringing a blazer onboard – it's nice to dress up for Captain's dinners or other more formal functions. Looking spiffy at check-in might even prompt an upgrade. One fancy outfit is all that's needed, but it will come in handy for date nights or special outings.

CARRY-ON IS QUEEN

You're flying to Miami for a seven-day cruise, but your checked luggage decides to visit Phoenix. Opt for a carry-on bag when flying instead, to avoid mishaps, and use the smaller size as a gauge to measure how much clothing you should bring on your trip. A week's worth of cold-weather clothing will indeed fit in a large carry-on if you're a prudent packer, as will two weeks of warm-weather gear. If you absolutely have to upgrade to a larger suitcase, the items in the sidebar should remain on your

person in a small bag or satchel when you board the plane.

STICK OUT FROM THE CROWD

Raise your hand if you have a black suitcase. (You probably raised your hand, right?) Black's a great choice – sleek and streamlined – but it can also lead to a lot of confusion. Imagine the luggage holding room on a megaship with its 6000 black bags – someone might mistake your bag for their own, or vice versa. Add a distinguishing mark like a colourful ribbon to your suitcase to avoid any mix-ups. Having the airline put a "fragile" sticker on your bag works as well, and it might help prevent your stuff from getting chucked around.

Your passport, credit card, camera, phone charger, power adapter, iPad and so on should stay with you at all times during transit.

Two Days' Worth of Clothing
Remember, if your suitcase misses the boat, you probably won't see it until the end of your trip. A pair of versatile pants (or a dress), a bathing suit, two undergarments, and two tops will cover the basics.

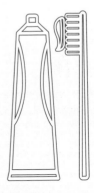

Essential Toiletries
Bring some minis, like a travel toothbrush, deodorant, a moisturising sunscreen, hand sanitiser, and – of course – any medication.

THE CRUISE HANDBOOK

CRUISE ETIQUETTE

Five Commandments to Be Your Best Self on Board

1. Thou shall practice conscious onshore etiquette. Remember, when on the road you are a cultural ambassador representing not only yourself but your home country or town. Be respectful. Be curious but kind. And read up on local customs – cultural dos and don'ts – before your trip.

2. Thou shall not treat the entire ship as your own home. Private and public spaces on cruises (ie your cabin versus the rest of the ship) are clearly demarcated, so treat the public spaces as such.

Doing so respects your fellow passengers. Cruises are about being comfortable, not infringing on other people's comfort.

3. Thou shall be a respectful audience member. If you're on a ship that has performances, whether musicals, comedy hours, live bands or even science lectures, treat the gathering and onstage talent as you would at a show on land. Just because the entertainment is "free" due to being included in the price of the cruise is no reason to be less respectful.

Don't come and go at inopportune times and refrain from chatting during a performance.

4. Thou shall tip. You may already be tipping and don't even know it – most major cruise lines have built 15%, 18% or 20% gratuities directly into your payments. (It's best to verify before your trip.) Even though tipping is largely an American concept, ship crews generally don't make a lot of money, and additional income can go a long way for exceptional service, especially for employees from countries where the GDP is lower than developed nations.

5. Thou shall retreat to your cabin when unwell. If you're feeling under the weather and decide to visit the medic, they will immediately send you back to your cabin if they're worried you might be contagious. If your vacation plans are being side-lined by an upset stomach and a sore throat, be considerate and limit your contact with other passengers. Remember: they're on a hard-earned vacation, too. If you're seasick and about to throw up, find a restroom or head back to your cabin. No one's interested in seeing what you ate for dinner!

IT'S A **SHIP**

ALPHA !

OSCAR !

ECHO !

LiNGO

Learn how to talk like a sailor, without the swear words.

Is it a ship or a boat?
A ship is a vessel large enough to carry a smaller nautical craft, and a boat is small enough to fit on a larger vessel.

SHIP LINGO 101
What to know before you go.
Aft The onboard back of the ship
Bow The front of the ship
Bridge Where the commanding crew controls the ship

Draft How deep the ship goes below the waterline
Galley The ship's kitchen
Knot A speed measurement (roughly 1.15 miles or 1.85 km per hour)
Muster The act of assembling in a designated area
Muster station The chosen point where passengers and crew assemble upon request
Port The left side of the ship when facing the front of the vessel (also portside)
Starboard The right side of the ship when facing the front of the vessel

Stern The offboard back of the ship
Tender A small water-craft used to ferry passengers from ship to shore
Windward The side of the ship exposed to the wind

SECRET CODES
A shortlist of signals that the cruise crews don't want you to know!
Alpha A medical emergency
Bravo A fire
Charlie A security threat
Delta A suspected biohazard
Echo Potential damage

to the ship's physical integrity (collision or intense wind)
Kilo Crew to report to muster points
Oscar Man overboard
Zulu Altercation among passengers

ZULU !

EXCURSiONS

Shore excursions can largely be broken down into three types, sightseeing, cultural and active, and they range in size from private guided outings to large group tours of more than 50 travellers. The beauty of the excursion is that they can be mixed and matched in so many configurations that you could take the same cruise twice and have completely different experiences each time.

On large cruises with a beach and relaxation focus, oftentimes you're choosing between lounging on the sand free of charge, a short-commitment sports experience (parasailing, scuba diving) or a scenic tour like visiting Mayan ruins. Small ship cruising with an expedition or adventure focus (such as Lindblad Expeditions) most always have their excursions neatly rolled into the price of your booking. Midsized ships tackling destinations with a cultural bent will have a plethora of onshore activities available at an extra charge, but may not have oodles of amenities to keep you satisfied on board if you opt out. This is when planning your own off-ship experiences ahead of time is key to getting the most of your cruise.

TONY CARNE'S TOP ACTIVITIES

Miami: Instead of the beach, try some Cuban food and take a salsa dance class.
Venice: Rather than being crushed by crowds in San Marco Square, go across the Grand Canal and try the traditional *cicchetti apertivo*.
Vienna: Skip museums and check out one of the city's traditional coffee shops.
Santo Domingo: Instead of sightseeing crumbling landmarks, visit a boutique rum distillery and take a chocolate-making class.
Crete: Instead of wandering Heraklion, go full-on foodie with Cretan cuisine.

Six things to bring on your DIY shore excursion

1. A small portable charger for your mobile phone.

2. The address of your ship's port written on a piece of paper in case you get lost.

3. An unlocked mobile phone with international calling capabilities.

4. A small amount of cash in the local currency.

5. A light bag to carry your belongings and new souvenir acquisitions.

6. A filled water bottle, especially when you're in a port without potable water.

Tony Carne, the managing director of Urban Adventures (www.urbanadventures.com), offers his advice on booking the best onshore experiences and excursions while cruising:

"With some advanced planning before your cruising adventure begins, you can book a private or even custom experience for the price of a big bus tour run by the cruise line. There are plenty of reliable operators unaffiliated with the cruise line that regularly pick up passengers at the ports for bespoke tours – you'll find them just beyond the disembarkation terminal. Strongly consider using a reputable company with an online presence, as you'll want to make sure they're properly

Clockwise from left: Exploring Venice; Santo Domingo at twilight; a pick-me-up for sightseeing in a Viennese cafe

insured to bring travellers around. Selecting a locally based guiding service will ensure that your purchases are directly stimulating the local economy. And if you want to go at it alone, opt for public transportation – you'll see way more of the city on the metro or tram than you would from the window of your tour bus."

THINK OUTSIDE THE SHIP

Your holiday doesn't need to live and die by your cruise's itinerary – consider extending your trip before and/or after your time on the water.

CRUISETOURS

You may want to marinate a little bit longer in the destinations you're visiting by cruise. That's why many travellers are keen on extending their stay before or after a cruise in their port of call – and why cruising companies provide deals with their affiliated hotels. Some like Royal Caribbean have even created tailored cruisetours that combine the best of seafaring and by-land experiences. If you don't want the full-on package experience, but plan on spending a long weekend in Quito before boarding your boat in the Galapagos, hanging out in Barcelona before taking a spin through the Mediterranean, or drinking copious amounts of Starbucks in Seattle before climbing up towards Alaska, you can still contact your cruise (or travel agent) to see what kinds of perks they can offer, including discounted accommodation, food vouchers and free transportation.

5 WELL-ESTABLISHED CRUISETOUR CHOICES

1. Canada's Rockies Tack on a week in Banff and Whistler after your Alaskan cruising foray.

2. Japan's Temple Towns Sail around the Land of the Rising Sun, then dip inland to explore the nation's hidden shrines.

3. Ireland's Interior Explore the epic Ring of Kerry after taking in the island's craggy cliffs from sea.

4. Peru's Lost Empires The South American coast starkly contrasts the secret ruins of the Incan Empire high up in the Andes.

5. Australia's Outback Sail into Sydney, the most stunning urban harbour in the world, then travel deep into the Red Centre to experience its sandy desolation.

CREATE YOUR OWN MULTI-STOP TRIP

If you purchased a cruise by itself (no bundling with hotels or flights), then you can easily dovetail other elements onto either end of your boat journey. When tacking on your own travel to/from your cruise, it's best to conceive of the entirety of your trip as one piece. This is an opportunity to hit must-sees within range of your port of embarkation. If the cruise is the centerpiece of your holiday, then plunk it into your planning accordingly – in the middle of your calendar. Try to save any flights to nearby sights for after you disembark, so you don't have to worry about airline delays keeping you from your cruise. Most port cities are well-provisioned with transit options for you to continue your jouney onwards; take advantage and you can get two vacations on one trip. Don't forget when planning that you may need a deceleration at the end of your journey, so you feel revitalised by the holiday and not desperately needing another to recover from the nonstop pace.

Left: Driving into Australia's Northern Territory; Above: Key Largo is an easy trip from most Florida cruise ports

PORT OF MIAMI / PORT EVERGLADES
Take a 90-minute drive from the quiet shores of Key Largo to snorkel in the placid waters of John Pennekamp Coral Reef State Park.

PORT OF COZUMEL
Ferry yourself to the mainland for a 50-minute drive to the hipster-hippie commune of Tulum where sand and rainforest collide into Mayan ruins.

PORT OF BARCELONA
From this Catalunya capital, roll down to the nearby coastal town of Sitges for its fun, European beach vibe minus the cruise crowds.

PORT OF CIVITAVECCHIA
Since Rome's main port of call is the gateway to this must-see Italian capital, indulge in a proper Roman holiday before boarding your boat, or venture an hour up the coast to the quieter town of Porto Santo Stefano.

PORT OF ST THOMAS
Get thee to St John, just a short ferry ride away, an island covered almost entirely by a national park and the perfect escape on a Caribbean cruise.

THE CRUISE HANDBOOK

iNSPiRATiON

TOP 10 AFFORDABLE CRUISE OPTIONS

Which destinations are affordable changes throughout the year in reaction to annual travel trends. Take advantage to get great deals by leveraging some of the below tactics.

TRAVEL OFF-SEASON

The best way to hit up the most popular cruising destinations on the planet at a fraction of the typical cost is to select a sail date outside of high season. Fares follow projected weather patterns, meaning that off-season or low season fares cannot guarantee the most ideal weather – but with fares being half the price, it's worth checking out. Besides, you could luck into some serious sunshine. The cheapest months for the top cruise destinations are:

1. ALASKA
in May or September

2. EUROPE
in February or March

3. EASTERN CARIBBEAN
in August

BOOK OLDER MODELS

Just like we gravitate towards the latest iPhone and dream of signing up for one of those fancy Teslas, cruisers want everything that's shiny and new: bigger cabins, upgraded amenities and modernised ship layouts. But selecting an older ship often yields some of the best deals in the industry. Get the input of a travel agent and scout out three- or four-day itineraries on older, smaller vessels in the following destinations:

4. THE BAHAMAS

5. MEXICO

6. WESTERN CARIBBEAN

7. CUBA

REPOSITIONING SAIL

In order to maximise their profitability, cruise companies will move their vessels from one region to another to capitalise on the alternating high seasons around the globe. As they move from one place to the next, cruise companies bring passengers along for the journey to defray the cost of reorienting their ships. Generally these trips have more time at sea and an always lower price tag. The three most common repositioning itineraries are:

8. CARIBBEAN TO EUROPE
across the Atlantic Ocean

9. ALASKA TO CALIFORNIA
along Canada and America's western coast

10. CALIFORNIA TO FLORIDA
through Central America and the Panama Canal

See p. 30 for tips and tricks on how to allocate funds on your upcoming adventure.

Clockwise from top left: The cathedral in Cologne on the Rhine; passing through the Panama Canal; spotting classic cars in Cuba; reef life in the Caribbean

65

TOP 10 BEACH CRUISE DESTINATIONS

Dip into the inviting waters of these bewitching beaches.

Left: The bungalows of Bora Bora; Right: In the Greek Mediterranean

1 SOCIETY ISLANDS, FRENCH POLYNESIA

Is there a more beautiful beach region on the planet? Moorea is flanked by soft sand, easily accessible to the public, Huahine feels wonderfully wild and unspoiled, and Bora Bora takes the prize for waters that shimmer with an uncanny shade of blue. Try a Paul Gauguin cruise to explore in depth.

2 GRAND TURK, TURKS & CAICOS

Some of the Caribbean's finest beaches are found in this quiet archipelago of 40 low-lying coral islands. Cruises usually dock at Grand Turk, where Governor's Beach awaits you with its crystal waters and white sand.

3 ARUBA

Aruba is blessed with such prototypical tropical beaches that you might think you're dreaming. Try Arashi Beach for an ideal snorkeling trip, Mangel Halto for a glimpse of mangrove habitat, or Eagle Beach for pristine white sands.

4 RIVIERA MAYA

Mexico's Yucatan region has Caribbean beaches with amazing food and Mayan temples to boot. Cozumel, Tulum, and Playa del Carmen each offer their own delightful mix of attractions, but they share gorgeous beach access.

5 GREEK ISLES

Lined with volcanic sand and set against a backdrop of whitewashed towns, the Greek islands offer a huge number of beaches to visit – with some amazing scenery. Crystal clear waters, tranquil coves and the sense of history lurking on the islands themselves all lend an ineffable touch to sunbathing and swimming, whether on Santorini, Corfu, Crete or Mykonos, to name just a few. Summer is the high season here and the number of itineraries available means there's something for every taste and budget. Raise a glass of grappa to that!

Left: Tulum on the Riviera Maya

9 VANUATU

Vanuatu's Champagne Beach will give you a sensation of luxurious celebration appropriate to its name. The island is so telegenic that *Survivor* even filmed here in a testament to the stunning island chain's castaway quality.

6 BRAZIL

No wonder Brazilians practically worship the beach when their country has one of the largest and most inspired coastlines on the planet, from the hideaway islands of Fernando de Noronha to the perfectly arcing bay of Lopes Mendes beach on Ilha Grande near Rio de Janeiro.

8 SEYCHELLES

This archipelago off the coast of East Africa in the Indian Ocean has gorgeous sifted-sand beaches and a host of endemic species protected by nature reserves. Most cruises are smaller luxury yachts, but if you're budget-minded you can island hop via the local ferryboats. If you're tired of the same old beach destinations, this exotic locale offers an exciting new experience.

10 INDONESIA

Bali, Java, Komodo and Sumatra – even the names of Indonesia's favorite destinations inspire dreaming of distant shores and crumbling temples. Bali is often included in Asian and Australian cruise itineraries.

CRUISE WEBSITE SEAHUB (www.seahub.com) studied over 1.8 million cruise-related posts on Instagram and determined that the most liked cruising destinations in the world were The Bahamas, Florida, and the Eastern Caribbean. Greece, Croatia, Australia, California and Mexico received honorable mentions.

7 CANARY ISLANDS

The shoreline along Spain's Canary Islands is one of the most visited by sunseekers from colder European climes. And why not? With nature resorts, sand dunes and surfing, the Canary Islands offer a variety of ports of call and beautiful beaches. Some are more secluded than others, but each has its own unique flavor. Plus, warm sunny weather is the norm year-round.

THE CRUISE HANDBOOK

TOP 10 CRUISES WITH VIEWS

These world-class destinations promise picture-postcard scenery.

2 NEW ZEALAND

With stunning natural beauty throughout the South Island, especially within the boundaries of Fiordland National Park, New Zealand lures in devotees with the scenery that drew in Andrew Jackson. A visit to Milford Sound is the undoubted capstone experience.

3 THE ARCTIC

In the far reaches of the Arctic Circle you can experience three bucket list sights in one day of sightseeing: the Aurora Borealis, polar bears and icebergs. Visits to Greenland's eastern coast reveal inlets and settlements visited by the first European explorers only a mere century ago.

4 SOUTH GEORGIA ISLAND

Teeming South Georgia Island is a massive breeding ground for seals and penguins, offering visitors one of the most gripping safari experiences on the planet. You won't soon forget the sight of the more than 300,000 king penguins on its shores.

5 HAWAII

The 50th US state gets top ranks when it comes to looks. A visit by sea instead of land opens up secret coasts inaccessible to land travellers, like Kauai's Na Pali with its signature mountain ridges that rise up like the spine of a sleeping dinosaur.

Clockwise from top left: Norway's fjords invite your awe; Na Pali Coast State Park; polar bears in the Arctic

1 NORWAY'S FJORDS

You'll be hard-pressed to find a more beautiful destination on the planet than Norway's fjords as they carve in and out of the coast. Each bit of land hides deep coves carved out by ancient glaciers, and the further north you go, the more dramatic each vista becomes.

6 HA LONG BAY

Few places capture the imagination – and Instagram "likes" – more than Vietnam's iconic collection of limestone towers that rise up from the depths of the ocean like breaching whales. Old teak barges with their fluttering, canvas sails add to the drama of the scene.

7 CROATIA

The Dalmatian Coast sparkles along the Adriatic Sea, with dramatic craggy cliffs sharing real estate with pine forests and pristine beaches. Still off the beaten path, its historic towns provide majestic scenery from the water and you're sure to fall in love with each new vista.

8 FAROE ISLANDS

These North Atlantic stunners offer impossibly beautiful scenery – tiny hamlets hemmed in between undulating waves of mountains. Isolated and unique, they are all the more special for being so remote.

9 MARQUESAS ISLANDS

Hidden in the corner of French Polynesia, the region's low-lying coral atolls suddenly burst forth towards the sky in the Marquesas – a collection of volcanic jungles and sharp stone. Sparsely populated but with a distinct cultural flavor, these Polynesian islands transport visitors back to the South Pacific of years gone by.

10 ST PETERSBURG

Baltic cruises sail by a plethora of impressive cities, but save the most striking – the cupola-covered St Petersburg – for last. Cathedral towers swoosh and swirl, palaces glimmer with bright colours and canals cut arteries through opulent residential blocks. A Russian city with European flare, St Petersburg doesn't disappoint.

Clockwise from top left: Ha Long Bay's karsts; puffins in the Faroe Islands; Church of the Savior in St Petersburg; a promenade along the Dalmatian Coast

THE CRUISE HANDBOOK

TOP 5 FOR KIDS, TWEENS & TEENS

Onboard youth programs with arts and crafts are featured on every megaship, but the best destinations for families are spots where activities can continue onshore.

2 ST THOMAS

There's probably no island in the Caribbean that packs more activities onto its shores than St Thomas. Try zip-lining and parasailing, or take the Skyride gondola to Paradise Point. Day passes to some of the island's hotels are available to give your daily pool party ritual a bit of variation.

3 TAURANGA

There's something for every interest in New Zealand's Bay of Plenty. Any *Lord of the Rings* fans in the family will love seeing the Hobbiton set at Tauranga, as well as the Māori villages and incredible geothermal activity in Rotorua.

4 HAWAII

Hang ten along the shores of the Aloha State, where you can snorkel with turtles, try a surfing tutorial, or let your culturally curious kids engage in some of the local traditions, thoughtfully distilled into colourful classes taught by local ambassadors.

5 ALASKA

Alaska has something for every age, with tons of active excursions. The megaship cruises in the region attract so many families that itineraries are geared to keeping them happy. Plus every age will love experiencing the rugged glacial coast.

1 BAHAMAS

If you're touching land anywhere near Paradise Island, head straight to Atlantis where day-trippers can purchase a pass to its massive waterpark facility that fuses together kid fun such as waterslides and over-water jungle gyms with plenty of amenities.

Clockwise from top: The St Thomas cruise port; exploring Hawaii; Pioneer Park in Fairbanks, Alaska; Paradise Island in the Bahamas

Opposite page, left to right: Budapest on the Danube; a Mexico beach

TOP 5 SHORT CRUISES

*Can't get away for that transoceanic crossing but still yearning to set sail?
With two-, three-, and four-night cruise options available from a variety of ports,
you can find a long weekend getaway to satisfy your craving.*

1 BERMUDA

Easily accessible from the East Coast, a quick jaunt to Bermuda offers cruisers all the usual onboard temptations, from comedy shows to gambling, set against a tantalising backdrop of turquoise water.

2 THE DANUBE

The four-day, abridged version of this classic river tour takes in Vienna and Budapest alongside smaller towns, ideal for weekenders who want different views (and countries) out their window while on board. A Danube cruise does an admirable job of soaking up the best its destinations have to offer.

3 MEXICO

It feels as though the entire Riviera Maya of Mexico features one unwavering ribbon of sand. A three-day itinerary hugs the coastline with each stop offering passengers the opportunity to chow down on top-notch tacos or suit up for some scuba diving.

4 SYDNEY TO MELBOURNE

Instead of negotiating the 10-plus hours of dusty highway between Australia's two biggest cities, consider sailing along the coastline over the course of a weekend. Small bays, lonely beaches and dramatic cliffs punctuate the shore, with a handful of townships breaking up the desolation.

5 NOWHERE

Yes, you read that correctly – sometimes it's nice to get away without the destination being the primary objective. A handful of days on the water can feel like a fun, Vegas-at-sea weekend with plenty of pool time and innumerable entertainment options.

LGBTQ

Specifically LGBTQ cruises are run by third-party charter operators such as Atlantis and Olivia. Off the ship, here are five top ports to fly the rainbow flag. The International Gay & Lesbian Travel Association (www.iglta.org) is another great resource.

1 KEY WEST

The motto of Key West is "One Human Family," and it's long been known as a gay getaway for its accepting, inclusive atmosphere.

2 MYKONOS

Mykonos has created a uniquely open and friendly culture that makes it a must for any LGBTQ bucket list.

3 LISBON

From its beaches to the bars and clubs of Chiado, Bairro Alto, and Principe Real, Lisbon have a vibrant LGBTQ scene that extends far beyond its annual Pride Parade.

4 PUERTO VALLARTA

The so-called "San Francisco of Mexico" has a dedicated LGBT Business & Tourism Association and a long-established history as the most gay-friendly destination in all of Mexico, with nightlife aplenty.

Above: The harbour of Mykonos; Top right: Celebrants at Sydney's Mardi Gras; Left: Socialising in Key West

5 SYDNEY

As befits a city world-famous for its annual Gay and Lesbian Mardi Gras, Sydney has a long-established queer scene with something for everyone.

GAY WEDDINGS

Hearing wedding bells? With the 2017 legalization of gay marriage in Malta, all Celebrity Cruises – whose ships are registered in the island nation – can perform legally recognised gay weddings on board.

TOP FOODIE DESTINATIONS

If you're a foodie looking for inspiring meals on your cruise, these spots represent some of the best bets around the globe. Consider signing up for a themed culinary cruise with cooking classes and lectures on board.

- Bordeaux, France
- Copenhagen, Denmark
- Hong Kong, China
- Tuscany, Italy

CULTURE CRUISE DESTINATIONS

These cruises to historic, vibrant destinations will expand your cultural horizons.

1. Japan No country on the planet swirls together its rich history and striking modernity more adeptly than Japan. The Land of the Rising Sun rivets visitors with an incredibly distinct sense of place, from its ancient temples – some of the largest wooden structures on the planet – to its bustling urban intersections among neon lights. Cruise out of Osaka, Tokyo, Nagoya or Kobe and experience a country like no other.

2. Nile River Some things never go out of style, like the extravagant tombs and pyramids erected thousands of years ago in honor of the Pharaohs. Despite the sands of time, these sentinel monuments remain steadfast where the Saharan desert's orange waves reach the fertile shores of the Nile. Visit Luxor and the Valley of the Kings by river cruise to get up close to these ancient monuments.

3. Eastern Mediterranean The vibrant trade routes along the Mediterranean created rich, cross-pollinated cultures that continue to echo around us today. Testaments of these ancient societies stand watch from the ruins of temples, amphitheaters, citadels and bathhouses, bleached white by the warm Mediterranean sun.

4. India Relish a slice of life in the world's second-most populous country by cruising the backwaters of Kerala, a calm antidote to some of the busier corners of India. Glide down the rivers in a kettuvallam, a traditional houseboat used to transport goods from one village to the next – and enjoy a place unmarred by industrialism and unworried by Instagram "likes."

5. British Isles Live out your Harry Potter fantasies by cruising from cathedral to crumbling castle as you wend your way around England, Wales, Scotland and Ireland. From the long sands of Cornwall through the craggy edges of the Pembrokeshire Coast and up into the stark and stunningly desolate isles of the Outer Hebrides, the UK is as eye-catching as it is culturally rich.

TOP 10 ADVENTURE CRUISES

Set sail on an adrenaline-filled expedition to one of these thrilling locales.

1) AMAZON

The planet's most primordial and impenetrable rainforest is only accessible along its tributaries, and the river cruises that ply its waters reveal an unusual world of singing birds, shy manatees, playful pink dolphins, elusive sloths and colourful plant life.

2) MYANMAR

River cruising along the Irrawaddy between Mandalay and the countless temples of Bagan offers the perfect marriage of postcard-worthy landscapes and a rich cultural heritage. Local food and art round out the completely immersive experience.

3) BOTSWANA

Africa's latest tourist trend is wildlife watching from a boat instead of a safari car. Cruise the Chobe River or slide through the Okavango Delta in search of grazing elephants, sleeping lions or marauding hyenas.

4) SVALBARD

A no-man's-land above the Arctic Circle, Svalbard is technically governed by Norway, but is halfway to the North Pole! Its remote location is ideal for adventurers keen to climb through glacial caves and more.

5) PATAGONIA

At the southernmost tip of South Africa, the striking glacial landscape of Patagonia tempts active cruisers with zodiac excursions amid the fjords and whale watching from a kayak seat. Sailing Cape Horn, the Drake Passage and the Strait of Magellan puts you in the wake of legendary seafarers of yore.

Left: The Amazon in Brazil; Center: In the ice at Svalbard; Above: A Commerson's dolphin in Patagonia; Opposite page, left: The Avenue of the Baobabs; Opposite page, center: A walking path in the Azores

6 MADAGASCAR

Sometimes known as the Eighth Continent for its sheer size (roughly the same as France) and volume of unique biodiversity, Madagascar feels worlds apart from the rest of the planet. Coastal cruises can access the towering baobab trees (some of the oldest living beings on the planet) and untouched archipelagos of offshore islets. River cruises take to the island's jungly interior and get up close and personal with the endemic species found there.

7 KAMCHATKA

There are wild frontiers, and then there's Kamchatka, a massive peninsula dangling off Russia's Far East. Frequented by rugged expedition vessels, this undeveloped expanse features thick taiga forests of pine and brooding volcanoes that rise out of the Pacific Ring of Fire. Keep your eyes peeled for the brown bears native to the region.

8 AUSTRALIA

Australia's population is almost entirely found along its coastal edges, concentrated in a handful of large cities. That leaves the wild and remote corners of the country, like the Kimberley Coast or Ningaloo Reef, almost untouched and ripe for exploration.

9 PITCAIRN

One of the most remote inhabited islands on the planet, Pitcairn was settled by the mutineers of the infamous HMS *Bounty* in 1790, whose descendants – around 50 people – still live on the island to this day. A green fleck in the ocean, this is the ultimate destination for adventure seekers who can visit by cargo freighter or stop for the day on the specialty cruises plying the remote Pacific waters each year.

10 AZORES

A popular pit stop for transatlantic cruises, the Portuguese archipelago of nine islands with stunning, dramatic outcrops were formed by tumultuous volcanic activity millions of years ago. The rich Azorean culture, traditional Iberian food and brine-tinged wine add further rewards to sailing around these verdant isles.

TOP 5 DIVE DESTINATIONS

Fancy yourself a scuba-holic? These liveaboard cruises let you go full-blown Cousteau.

1. RAJA AMPAT AND KOMODO, INDONESIA
Despite very seasonal conditions, western Indonesia features some of the most robust diving in the world.

2. MALDIVES
Why not tour the atolls while sleeping on a small cruiser?

3. PALAU
Palau's sites are far offshore, making liveaboards more efficient for getting around.

4. COCOS ISLAND, COSTA RICA
Swim with hundreds of scalloped hammerheads.

5. SIMILAN ISLANDS, THAILAND
This national park frontier offers backpacker prices.

OFF-THE-BEATEN-TRACK CRUISES

Filippos Venetopoulos, the general marine manager of Peregrine Adventures (www. peregrineadventures. com), offers his top picks for the best off-the-beaten-path options around the world from wildlife cruises to purely scenic passages.

1 VIETNAM

While river cruises along the Mekong River have become very popular in recent years, try the newly emerging trend of travelling along the coastline from Hanoi to Ho Chi Minh City. The experience offers miles of untouched coast and vistas beheld only by local fishermen.

Clockwise from top right: The Seychelles at sunset; dock diving in Cape Verde; The Senegal River

2 THE GALAPAGOS

An adventure cruise in the Galapagos offers the condensed history of evolution rolled into one microcosm. These faraway islands have become quite popular over the last two decades, yet the island chain still feels wild and wonderfully untouched.

3 WEST AFRICA

A great choice for second-time travellers to the continent, cruising the rivers of West Africa in Senegal and Gambia offers a compelling mixture of history, culture and incredible wildlife viewing. Break the mold by opting for a safari by cruise instead of by land, and consider this region for your animal photography instead of Southern or East Africa.

4 THE SEYCHELLES

A truly remote experience, the Seychelles are located far off the east coast of Africa in the middle of the Indian Ocean. Cruises that take in its small islands offer incredible beachside experiences

and unmatched bird watching. Explore centuries-old rainforests, impossibly clear lagoons and quaint island communities.

5 CAPE VERDE

This stunning volcanic archipelago is known for its Creole culture which mixes Portuguese and African flavors. Don't miss the opportunity to experience the local morna music, and relax on one of the seemingly endless beaches.

ON THE RISE

Filippos Venetopoulos shares his picks for the top under-the-radar cruising destinations that are trending up.
- Costa Rica
- Panama
- Iceland
- The Black Sea
- The Kimberley Coast, Australia

SELF-CRUISING DESTINATIONS

Ian Pedersen, sailing expert and product manager for The Moorings (www.moorings.com) picks the best places in the world to charter your own vessel.

 **1. British Virgin Islands** Often dubbed the sailing capital of the world, the British Virgin Islands are ideally suited for yacht charter vacations. The constant breeze of the trade winds, balmy temperatures year-round easily navigable waters, and abundance of natural harbours draw in sailing enthusiasts from around the world. There are over 60 islands to choose from, so you can come back year after year.

 **2. Croatia** Once the best-kept secret of the sailing community, Croatia has rapidly grown into the most popular cruising destination in Europe, thanks to its dramatic geography, unique culture and world-class cuisine. The Dalmatian Coast is dotted with hundreds of islands easily explored from the deck of your own yacht.

 **3. Greek Islands** It goes without saying that the Greek Isles are a bucket-list destination for most travellers, and similar to Croatia, a day trip on a ferry simply won't do. Set sail from Athens and transport yourself back in time as you explore temples, ruins and stone-carved towns clinging to the sides of cliffs. Arriving by sailboat, you'll soak in the beauty and ambiance of the Mediterranean Sea.

 **4. French Polynesia** One of the most iconic and exotic sailing destinations in the world, French Polynesia is a sailor's paradise. Forget staying in the over-water bungalows of Bora Bora – the only way to truly see the region is by boat. Don't miss the lesser-known Society Islands like Raiatea, Taha'a and Huahine, settled centuries ago by brave, seafaring explorers from far away.

 **5. The Windward Islands** Encompassing hundreds of islands from Martinique down to Grenada, this area represents a step up in both beauty and difficulty from other parts of the Caribbean. It's the only destination on the list with some open-water sailing. The lesser-known islands of Bequia, Carriacou, and the Tobago Cays promise pristine natural beauty both above and below the waves.

See p. 36 for everything you need know about organising a private boat journey.

CHOOSE YOUR
CRUISE

LIFESAVER TIP

ON LONGER JOURNEYS, DECORATE YOUR CABIN WITH TOUCHES FROM HOME, AND CONSIDER BRINGING A HANDS-ON PROJECT AND YOUR FAVORITE COMFORT FOOD.

○ Culture

◐ Food

◔ Relaxation

ROUND-THE-WORLD

Take the trip of a lifetime! Only a few dozen ships have authentic round-the-world itineraries, but hundreds of other ships cruise the planet with partial circumnavigations. No matter which you choose, you'll visit far-flung locales like Easter Island, Greenland, the South Pacific, St Helena or Madagascar.

Does being on the open ocean, with hardly any land in sight and plenty of time to read or enjoy some fresh air, sound like an exciting adventure? If you answered "yes," then a round-the-world cruise could be the perfect cruise for you.

While cruises are short flings, round-the-world circumnavigations are long-term commitments. World cruises that start and end in the same or nearby ports need, at the very least, 90 to 100 days to circle the globe, and a few cruise lines run 150-day (or more) circumnavigation cruises. These round-the-world adventures stop in no fewer than two dozen ports, and often up to 30, 40 or even 50 destinations. They generally hit about a dozen large, well-known cities such as Singapore, Cape Town, Mumbai, and San Francisco, and will stop in at least another dozen less-visited destinations from the Seychelles or Montenegro to Pitcairn Islands.

World-cruise passengers are very rarely first-timers, so these cruises cater to knowledgeable veterans who expect the best of the best. A circumnavigation

THE CRUISE HANDBOOK

three sections of the globe: Australasia and the South Pacific, for example, or South America and Antarctica. You can thus hop onto a round-the-world cruise for a segment of the journey rather than doing it from start to finish, getting the same open-ocean, intrepid-destination feel without committing as much time or money.

There are several other non-standard ways to get around the world on a ship. The first is a repositioning cruise. When a cruise ship based in Europe for the summer needs to head to South America for their winter cruises, the cruise line will often offer an extremely discounted cruise for this one-way journey. You might visit two to five ports

cruise could see almost half of its days at sea, so the focus is much more on the ship experience itself than most other cruises, including daily activities, fine dining (some cruises offer up to a half-dozen places to eat), spas, Broadway-style entertainment and casinos. Several lines bring inter-port lecturers and experts on board to help passengers learn about the culture, ecology or history of their next destination. As with all cruise liners, some are glitzy affairs with black-tie dinners, while others are more resort casual.

The longer itineraries cost well into five figures, but most people don't realise they can go on a portion of a world cruise that is far shorter and less expensive. Many cruise lines run 15- to 50-day partial world or transoceanic cruises. These traverse two or

Clockwise from top: The moai of Easter Island; an African penguin in Cape Town; the town of Tasiilaq in Greenland

SEMESTER AT SEA

Since 1963, this floating university has run semester-long sails around the globe, west to east in the fall, vice versa in the spring. Study Buddhism in a shipboard classroom on Tuesday, meet with monks in Kyoto, Japan on Wednesday. The 600 university students come from all over the world, but you don't have to be a student to sail; about 25 to 30 adult passengers join each semester and are welcome to audit classes.

CUNARD

This was the first company to offer round-the-world cruises in 1923, and its famed ships the *Queen*

CARRIER OPTIONS

Elizabeth, *Queen Mary II* and *Queen Victoria* luxury liners circumnavigate the globe every year. With grand lobby staircases, artistic touches reminiscent of Cunard's art deco history, and theatres that include private balcony seating, these cruises are the grand dame of luxury world cruising.

AZAMARA

New to the round-the-world cruise scene, the opulent Azamara World Journey sails in March from Sydney to London. It times its itinerary to land in port for some of the year's poshest events, from the Cannes Film Festival to the Monaco Grand Prix.

HIGHLIGHT

Cruising around the planet is a journey few humans have taken. The first known success was on Magellan's *Victoria* in 1521; though amenities have improved since then, this antidote to the whiplash-speed pace of today's world recalls days of exploring long past. One of the best parts of a round-the-world cruise is the romance of travelling by this oldest means of transport. Consider keeping a journal or starting a photography or art project you can share with loved ones back home.

Epic Cruise Experiences

Go from a pollywog to a shellback by order of King Neptune in a coconut bra. No, really. When crossing the equator for the first time, you'll be initiated into this old, sailor tradition, which very often includes kissing a fish! Newly-minted shellbacks receive an equator-crossing certificate.

—

Round-the-world cruises follow good weather and hug the tropics for weeks. For a nightcap like no other, watch magnificently long, pink and orange sunsets from the bow (or stern).

—

Sailing through the Panama Canal locks is a once-in-a-lifetime experience. This engineering marvel more than ten years in the making leaves even the most jaded visitor impressed as it crosses from the Pacific to the Atlantic Oceans.

THE CRUISE HANDBOOK

over 15 to 25 days, but at around half the cost of a traditional round-the-world cruise section.

Still not extreme enough for you? Consider booking a room on a working cargo or freighter ship – but bring your own entertainment, whether in the form of a travelling partner or a lot of books. There are no onboard activities or amenities and few other paying passengers, but this is an experience only a few hundred guests will have each year.

If, however, even a round-the-world cruise is too brief for you and your pockets are deep enough, the aptly named luxury liner *The World* has 165 private residences from studio cabins to three-bedroom suites with full kitchens. This ship cruises around the world indefinitely, stopping in rare expedition ports the resident owners vote for, including Antarctica and the Falkland Islands.

Key Port Feature

CAPE TOWN

Cape Town's location near the Cape of Good Hope ensures that it stays on the radars of world-cruise itineraries. It offers the perfect place to stretch your legs after days at sea. For an unbeatable view, take the cable car or brave the challenging hike up to the top of expansive Table Mountain, where you'll have a view of the confluence of the Indian and Atlantic oceans (though the exact point where the oceans merge may be slightly more to the east). Next get up close with the African penguin colony at Cape Town's Boulder Beach or admire the 3000 species of plants at Kirstenbosch Botanical Garden, acclaimed as one of the best in the world.

WHO'S IT FOR

Classic round-the-world cruises are made for people with quite a bit of time and money on their hands, so think well-heeled retirees or – more and more these days – middle-class couples who've given up mortgages to cruise semi-permanently. The other types of world cruising – Semester at Sea, repositioning cruises, cargo or freighter vessels – attract a more intrepid, younger crowd.

Left: Cape Town beckons;
Right: The Singapore skyline

Itinerary

18 DAYS

Can't spare the three-plus months for a full circumnavigation? An 18-day stretch will take you on a segment from Sydney to Singapore or Singapore to Dubai. In fact, segments can be easily customised at a number of lengths.

100 DAYS

Look beyond cities like Hong Kong, Cape Town, and San Francisco for itineraries that stop in harder-to-reach locations you might not see otherwise. Cunard stops in Mauritius, Reúnion and Tonga; Oceania visits Rangoon, Cyprus and the Falkland Islands.

THE CRUISE HANDBOOK

LIFESAVER TIP

ON A BUDGET? TRY A FERRY ON THE ALASKA Z MARINE HWY FOR A DIY CRUISE OF THE INSIDE PASSAGE.

ALASKA

Cruising in Alaska offers a window into a vast, primordial wilderness once only accessible to intrepid, highly-supplied explorers or fortune-hunters sick with gold fever. From the comfortable deck of the ship, you'll be treated to a memorable feast of calving glaciers, daunting mountains, majestic wildlife and the atmospheric ruins of mines from the Klondike Gold Rush.

Practicalities

🧳 Alaskan weather is fickle. Pack warm layers, durable rainwear, good walking shoes and a pair of binoculars to bring Alaska's stunning scenery into focus.

🚆 Seattle, Washington; Vancouver, BC; Anchorage, Alaska

📅 Alaska cruise ships set sail early May and close in September. July and August are the warmest, driest (and busiest) months. The region's shoulder season offers better prices in May and September, and there are no cruises in winter.

$ $ $

○ **Adventure**
○ Outdoors
◉ Culture

C ruise ships bound for Alaska usually zigzag their way up via the fabled Inside Passage, typically departing from Seattle or Vancouver. As the liners nudge north of the 55th Parallel, civilisation quietly dissolves away, and the landscape becomes progressively more rugged amid the dense number of islands and channels that make up the Alexander Archipelago. Over 1100 islands create a network of fjords, creating stunning views as well as protected sailing waters.

About a million cruisers enter this watery domain each summer season. If you're one of them, you'll be rewarded by candid views of foraging fauna and scattered off-the-grid communities adorned with Alaskan Native art and storm-scarred fishing boats. For a large portion of the voyage, you pass through the Tongass National Forest. Roughly the size of Ireland, it's the largest national forest in the US with a wild potpourri of mountains, glaciers, lakes, wetlands and aged trees. The bulk of the settlements in this neck of the woods have strong Native American ties and are only accessible by boat or plane. Indeed, apart from Juneau, Anchorage and Fairbanks, none of Alaska's towns count more than a few thousand inhabitants.

Ketchikan, the first Alaskan

Clockwise from left: Glacier Bay National Park; Denali National Park; kayaking in Glacier Bay National Park

THE CRUISE HANDBOOK

stop heading north, is a cruise ship town with a long history of salmon fishing. Beyond an assemblage of tourist shops lies the pleasantly disheveled and historic neighborhood, Creek Street, a myriad of Native American parks filled with the world's largest collection of totem poles, and a surfeit of sheltered coves and inlets crying out to be kayaked. Further north, you'll find roughshod Wrangell, a salt-of-the-earth outpost where dive bars reek of last week's spilled beer. Little-visited Petersburg harbours a traditional fishing village with a visible Norwegian heritage, and Sitka, once capital of Russian Alaska, showcases Alaska's Tlingit and Russian history in an expansive national park. Diminutive Haines is the best place in North America to view nesting bald eagles, and Skagway, at the head of the sheltered Lynn Canal, was once the epicenter of the 1897 Klondike Gold Rush and all its sideshows. Some cruise ships continue northwest across Prince William Sound to the bizarre Cold

Above: Taking the Polar Bear Plunge in Glacier Bay; Right: Glacial hiking

War outpost of Whittier.

Many ships offer cruisetours, allowing passengers to disembark in the port of Seward. Here you can take the Alaskan Railroad up to Anchorage and onto Denali National Park, the proverbial Serengeti of the North. If time allows, extend your cruise with a land excursion (whether booked directly or through the carrier) to give you a fuller experience of all Alaska has to offer.

Away from the ports, most

CARRIER OPTIONS

PRINCESS CRUISES Princess is the largest cruise company in Alaska, operating up to eight luxurious ships in any given season. Although the company sails all over the world, Alaska is deemed a Princess specialty. Most ships are relatively large, accommodating up to 3000 passengers with classy, un-gimmicky service and a decent array of food. On terra firma, Princess operates a small chain of upmarket wilderness lodges, railcars and motor coaches. Many of its packages offer cruisetours that provide side trips to Denali National Park and Fairbanks.

UNCRUISE ADVENTURES An antidote to the big liners, UnCruise offers themed 7- to 21-day cruises carrying 22 to 86 passengers that focus on watching wildlife, exploratory forays into Glacier Bay and adventure travel – think bushwhacking, paddle-boarding and glacier hikes. These small boats (or yachts) have modern, elegant staterooms, personal service and an onboard naturalist to teach you the ways of the Alaskan wilderness, and they also dock off-the-beaten-track in Wrangell and Petersburg. Most depart from Juneau or, more rarely, Seattle.

HIGHLIGHT

Alaska guards an estimated 100,000 glaciers covering an area approximately the size of Maryland. Glaciation isn't just an Ice Age legacy here, it's a process that's still occurring on the grandest of scales. Massive ice floes such as the Hubbard Glacier gouge out U-shaped valleys on their journey to the coast where they jettison huge icebergs into the ocean. Cruise ships

draw near some of these glaciers, but to get the chilliest of close-ups, jump on a jet-boat tour in Whittier, or take a bus to the Mendenhall Glacier Visitor Center near Juneau where you can snap on crampons and partake in a guided glacial hike.

Epic Cruise Experiences

Zip-line like a low-flying eagle above the forest canopy in Ketchikan.

—

Flightsee over cloud-enshrouded cliffs and powerful waterfalls in the Misty Fjords National Monument.

—

See black and brown bears foraging in their carefully protected, natural habitat at Pack Creek, Kodiak Island or Anan Wildlife Observatory.

—

Team up with a National Park guide for a walk through the former Klondike Gold Rush outpost of Skagway.

—

Kayak amid a placid patchwork of forested islands, sandy coves and rocky inlets in Sitka Sound.

THE CRUISE HANDBOOK

cruise ship itineraries incorporate a selection of southeast Alaska's unique watery highways: the Misty Fjords National Monument; the drippy, trippy Tracy Arm (another deep fjord and the best bet for seeing a glacier calve); and the icy heaven of Glacier Bay National Park, also known as the crown jewel of the Alaskan cruise industry. Glacier Bay epitomises the rugged allure of Alaska: towering glaciers, breaching pods of whales and the dangerously wild landscapes that give you an urgent sense of your own mortality – even from the safety of a comfortable cruise ship.

Key Port Feature

JUNEAU

Practically every cruise ship stops in the well-connected port of Juneau which, despite its daily deluge of tourists, manages to retain an authentic edge-of-the-wilderness flavor. Hemmed in by water on one side and steep velvety mountains on the other, this state capital is an excellent launching pad for a challenging day-hike or paddling excursion. The small, walkable town center preserves an ensemble of mining-era buildings along with a stash of bars and restaurants. Popular shore excursions include zip-lining on Douglas Island, flightseeing to the Taku Glacier Wilderness Lodge, ascending Mt Roberts via an aerial tram, or bussing north to the calving of Mendenhall Glacier.

WHO'S IT FOR

Cruising in Alaska attracts all types. Who wouldn't be besotted by such a vast array of dramatic scenery? Not surprisingly, seniors and families are particularly well represented, along with anyone who might struggle to access this vast feral wilderness on their own. Smaller ships, such as Lindblad-National Geographic Expeditions and UnCruise Adventures, attract more adventurous travellers, while the Disney fleet is ideal for families. The larger, more luxurious operators such as Princess Cruises and Carnival Cruises are favoured by mature couples and seniors.

Left: Quaint Ketchikan's waterfront;
Right: Mt Denali rises up in the interior

Itinerary

7 DAYS

The standard short itinerary sets out from Seattle or Vancouver before cruising up the Inside Passage via Canada to Ketchikan. Practically all the big liners stop in the ports of Ketchikan, Juneau and Skagway and provide generous day trips of Glacier Bay National Park. Some also stop in historic Sitka or in the purpose-built cruise port of Icy Strait Point.

14 DAYS

Longer one-way cruise itineraries take in all the same ports as a round trip cruise, but carry on past the Hubbard Glacier to Whittier on the edge of Prince William Sound before terminating in Seward. From here cruisetours can zip passengers by train up to Anchorage and Denali National Park for a chance to experience Alaska's wild interior.

THE CRUISE HANDBOOK

LIFESAVER TIP

NIGHTTIME IS ELUSIVE AT THESE LATITUDES DURING SUMMER, SO IF YOU NEED YOUR SHUT-EYE, PACK AN EYE MASK.

Practicalities

 Aberdeen, Scotland; Reykjavik, Iceland; Trømso, Norway; Helsinki, Finland; Murmansk, Russia.

💼 Layering is a must! Pack a base layer of high performance wool; a flexible, lightweight mid-layer for insulation; and a waterproof outer layer of pants, jacket and boots, and sunglasses for the brilliant northern sun.

📅 High Arctic journeys are confined to the northern summers from June to September when the pack ice recedes. Destinations further south can be reached earlier in May or later in October.

$ $ —— $ $ $ $

○ Adventure
○ Outdoors
○ Culture

ARCTIC

Vast, varied and vivid, the High Arctic offers a mystical adventure for ocean-loving travellers. Full of unusual wildlife, diverse scenery and fascinating cultures, you'll discover the North Pole's exciting, seafaring history, explore brilliant natural wonders and marvel at the teeming life on the edge of the ice.

The High Arctic stretches from the Russian Far East to the Norwegian Islands of Svalbard and on to Nunavut in Northern Canada. An expedition cruise vessel, whether a luxury ship or a research craft, is the ideal way to see the many offerings of the region.

Ships sail around Greenland to Eastern Canada or Iceland, navigating through archipelagos in search of polar bears and walrus. There is no better place to watch the sun circle the edges of the horizon than from the deck of the ship, as it casts its blazing pink hues across the snowy-white icebergs and glassy seas.

For those whose hearts are set on taking in the wildlife, take an Arctic safari in Spitsbergen, the largest island in the Svalbard archipelago. Under the shadow of its towering peaks, Spitsbergen houses roughly the same number of polar bears as it does humans. While you may not see as many giant icebergs, the constant stream of smaller ice floes are perfect for polar bears, walrus and arctic fox. Sightings of blue whales, bowhead whales and fin whales are also possible as the ship travels north.

If you'd like a glimpse into Arctic culture, a trip that includes the west coast of Greenland

Left: Northern fulmars soaring in Svalbard; Above: Traditional costume in Ilulissat, Greenland

THE CRUISE HANDBOOK

While Arctic ports are gateways to magical polar worlds, they tend to not be the most charming stops to explore. The exceptions are Bergen, Norway; Helsinki, Finland; and Reykjavik, Iceland.

BERGEN, NORWAY

The harbour of Bergen is full of beautifully preserved and colourful wooden houses, now protected as a UNESCO World Heritage sight.

HELSINKI, FINLAND

The natural setting and many parks in Helsinki add to its stunning architecture and intriguing dining scene.

REYKJAVIK, ICELAND

Reykjavik is the world's most northern capital, and it's filled with eye-popping design boutiques, a wild nightlife scene and quirky, creative people. The Blue Lagoon's geothermal hotspot is a special highlight.

Disko Island, off Greenland

HIGHLIGHT

This land of the midnight sun never disappoints. Stunning giants of sparkling, alabaster ice float elegantly through the waters. The sun circles the sky, dipping only to the edge of the horizon, but not past it, in the middle of the night, encasing you in a rosy-pink glow. These transcendent few hours, surrounded by the harsh and wild environment, beams beauty from every corner, inviting admiration for nature's power and grace.

WHO'S IT FOR

Wilderness seekers, adventure lovers and history enthusiasts will all marvel at a trip to the High Arctic. For centuries explorers searched for passages over the earth, and these voyages follow in their wake, filling each day with intimate wildlife encounters, stunning natural wonders and fascinating culture. History's echo rings across the water as whales glide gracefully past the ship and polar bears leap from ice floe to ice floe. Herds of walrus lounge on the ice clacking their tusks while seabirds soar overhead. Fjords, mighty glaciers and rocky peaks line the shores, draped with tiny, multihued flowers, making their brave, short appearance in a summer of endless days.

CARRIER OPTIONS

NATIONAL GEOGRAPHIC-LINDBLAD EXPEDITIONS
Of National Geographic-Lindblad's fleet, the *Orion* is custom-made for expedition cruising. Sophisticated and elegant, it provides accommodation for 106 passengers to explore the Bering Sea and Russia's Far East. Onboard naturalists and photographers will help broaden your adventure.

G ADVENTURES
The expedition ships of G Adventures explore Svalbard and Spitsbergen in search of polar bears – and are a bit more affordable. These cruises also offer kayaking options for those wanting to get out onto the water and power themselves through ice floes. Experts in wildlife and history even host lectures throughout the day.

QUARK EXPEDITIONS
A specialist in Arctic adventures, Quark will take you straight to the North Pole without looking back. As Arctic waters require, all vessels have been hull-strengthened; some of their fleet are even retired icebreakers. The latter may lack in luxury, but they make up for it in brute strength. Many ships include zodiacs to take out onto the icy waters.

offers stops in Qeqertarsuaq, one of Greenland's oldest towns. The relatively hip city Sisimiut has a fascinating museum, offering insight into the local culture and history of human habitation dating back 4500 years.

In Ilulissat you can marvel at the vast quantities of its magnificent icebergs calving from the Icefjord, one of the world's fastest moving

THE CRUISE HANDBOOK

Epic Cruise Experiences

Take out a kayak for an orca's-eye view of the sea ice and then paddle among the ice pack, utterly unlike anywhere else in the world.

—

Strap on your snowshoes and march across the ice into remote wilderness, with only the crunch of snow audible underneath.

—

Take a photography seminar paired with an extended shore excursion and let experts teach you how to get the best possible snap of that majestic polar bear.

and most active glaciers.

Where west Greenland is culturally rich, east Greenland is a naturalist's dream. Remote, spectacular and covered in ice, you'll watch the sun glisten off steep icebergs and flowing glaciers as the ship threads through mountains, fjords, glaciers and pack ice. Cruises often combine the Canadian High Arctic with Greenland to offer passengers more opportunities to witness the region's fascinating wildlife or learn about Inuit culture.

More remote still is the Russian Far East. Venture through the Bering Strait which separates the Asian and American continents and serves as a migratory channel for seabirds and whales. Disembark on Wrangel Island where blooms of wildflowers blanket the landscape, puffins nest in their hollows and musk ox and reindeer graze. Sightings of polar bears and walrus are also possible

depending on the state of the ice.

If you're an adventure seeker and bucket-list traveller, a trip through the Northwest Passage or to the North Pole might satisfy a dream of a lifetime. Seabirds, polar bears, whales and seals abound as the ship journeys steadily through the elusive passage connecting the Pacific and Atlantic Oceans. There you can see for yourself the courage that was needed of long-ago explorers, as you venture into overwintering sites, ceremonial grounds and ship graveyards.

The ultimate voyage may be to the most famous spot on the cap: 90 degrees north. A goal-oriented journey not easily accomplished, powerful icebreaker ships work themselves daily through the thick white ice to reach their destination. On board one of these monoliths, you will eventually arrive at the top of the world, stomp across the ice and snap a victorious photo.

Above & right: A polar bear; ice wall on Eqi Glacier; Opposite: Bergen, Norway

Itinerary

14 DAYS

From Helsinki you fly charter to Murmansk, Russia. The following day, you will begin your voyage north. From there you make a four-day journey through the Barents Sea with a good amount of whale watching. When you reach the polar ice cap, the ship cracks away at the pack ice, giving you time in the 24-hour daylight for a helicopter sightseeing tour. Once you reach the Pole and celebrate achieving your goal, your voyage heads south to explore Franz Josef Land, as well as discover polar bears and other wildlife that find sanctuary in Russian Arctic National Park. Finally you head back across the sea to disembark in Murmansk and charter-flight out the next day to Helsinki.

18 DAYS

Add a few days at the beginning or end of your North Pole expedition to tour Helsinki. Take advantage of the creature comforts of good food and boutique shopping in this quirky Finnish town.

THE CRUISE HANDBOOK

LIFESAVER TIP
SAIL FROM OCTOBER TO NOVEMBER OR FEBRUARY TO MARCH FOR A BETTER CHANCE AT SEEING THE NORTHERN LIGHTS AND A BIT OF SCENERY DURING DAYLIGHT HOURS.

BALTIC & NORWEGIAN COAST

Since the beginning of the Viking Age of longships, Scandinavians have been at sea. Baltic cruises give an overview of this beautiful and culturally diverse region, while Norwegian cruises take you into some of the world's grandest fjords and provide access to indigenous Sami culture.

Practicalities

 Stockholm, Sweden; Copenhagen, Denmark; Oslo, Norway; St Petersburg, Russia

🧳 Temperatures can be frigid so pack triple layers, thermals and heat-trapping boots and hats. In summer, endless sun means lots of sunscreen, too.

📅 Norwegian coastal cruises run year-round, but for cruising the Baltic Sea, the season is May to September. June through August sees the biggest crowds.

$ $ $

○ Culture
○ Outdoors
○ Food

WHO'S IT FOR

Most Baltic Sea cruises are extremely similar to ocean-going vessels in terms of size and amenities, but on these you can visit a half-dozen of some of the most expensive cities in the world for the price of a regular cruise. The clientele tends to be a bit more interested in culture and history. On Norwegian coastal cruises, passengers and the ships' itineraries are usually more active and adventurous.

Scandinavia and the Baltic Sea region are undeniably hot right now. Hygge, lagom, and lykke are all the rage, and our homes have long been dominated by the accessible modernist looks of Ikea furniture. The region's dining scene has made way for New Nordic cuisine and exotic Scandinavian liqueurs. So what are you waiting for?

Every major city in the Baltic Sea region is directly on the water, so cruisers can maximise every moment of the average eight-hour stop in port. All the Baltic Sea's port-city centers are fairly close to one another

THE CRUISE HANDBOOK

by sea, including Stockholm, Copenhagen, Oslo, Helsinki, Gdansk (Poland), Tallinn (Estonia) and Riga (Latvia) – where many residents speak perfectly fluent English. Cruises also travel to the notoriously difficult-to-visit St Petersburg, Russia's grandest city and a gilded window into a vast country. You don't need an expensive visa, and cruise ships often overnight there for two full days (sometimes three). In fact there are cost savings all over the place on a Baltic cruise. Baltic and Norwegian cruise prices are comparable to those in any other region, but you can see some of the world's most expensive cities for a relative bargain.

While the Baltic Sea is all about cosmopolitan, urbane cities, on a Norwegian coastal cruise, the top destination is the water. Ships sail up the western coast of Norway, past rushing waterfalls, blissful fjords and mountainous views, and slip through narrow waterways dripping with scenery. In winter the Norwegian coast is home to a range of once-in-a-lifetime experiences – seeing the Northern Lights, learning to drive a dogsled or riding in a reindeer-drawn sleigh.

Cruises on the fjords are simultaneously more relaxed and adventurous than most other cruises. One of the best pastimes on board is to serenely

HELSINKI

Finland is at the top of every world-happiness index, and a day in Helsinki will give you an idea of why. During the summer, the island fortress of Suomenlinna is one giant grassy park of museums and public space. Finnish design is all the rage these days, so check out the Design Museum, Contemporary Art Museum or some famous Finnish design shops. Along Esplanadi Park, you can browse Iittala glass (every Finnish house has their candy dish), Arabia pottery or Marimekko fabrics. To try reindeer sausage, pickled herring or organic forest blueberries, head to Hakaniemi Market.

Above & right: St Isaac's Cathedral in St Petersburg; smorgasbord with pickled herring; Opposite: Nyhavn Port in Copenhagen

Itinerary

7 DAYS

For a Baltic Sea cruise, you will typically embark from Stockholm, Copenhagen, Oslo or Amsterdam and visit all these cities, along with Helsinki, Gdańsk or Tallinn. You'll then dock in the most popular port of the cruise to visit St Petersburg, Russia. On a Norwegian cruise, you will sail out of Bergen (or Oslo) and up the western coastal fjords to Trondheim, Bodo, and Tromso.

14+ DAYS

These longer Baltic Sea cruises add more far-flung destinations – Warnemunde, Germany; Greenland; Iceland; Svalbard, Norway; northern Scotland and even the Faroe Islands. Several cruises stay in St Petersburg a full three nights. Some cruises combine the Baltic Sea and Norwegian coastal fjords or sail out of the UK.

watch for whales and waterfalls, but expeditions make the most of local winter sports. There is quite a bit of culture and history, as well, from Sami reindeer herders and the Arctic Cathedral in Trømso to Art Nouveau gem Alesund and ancient Viking sites. Some cruises even visit an ice bar or stop for an overnight in an ice hotel.

**Above: Majestic St Petersburg;
Right: The Northern Lights**

HIGHLIGHT

Visitors almost always need a visa to visit Russia, and acquiring it can be quite expensive and time consuming. One way around this visa is to take a cruise that stops in St Petersburg. Cruise lines cater to travellers who want to see Russia without the visa, and often spend one, two or even three full days in St Petersburg. The Hermitage Museum alone – the once-royal residence with its three million artifacts and pieces of art – needs an entire day. That's not to mention the gilded palaces and residences, ballet and folkloric performances, and stately domed cathedrals. Just remember: this is one Baltic stop where you'll need to book an organised tour, as passengers can't enter the city without one.

CARRIER OPTIONS

HOLLAND AMERICA

This cruise heavy-weight has partnered with *Food & Wine Magazine* for neo-Nordic cuisine shore excursions, like walking tours of Stockholm's farmers markets, Danish rye bread baking classes in Copenhagen or a Finnish restaurant that serves bear and reindeer meat alongside licorice ice cream.

NORWEGIAN CRUISE LINES

True to its name, Norwegian offers hundreds of Baltic Sea cruises a year for extremely reasonable prices. The Baltic Sea is one of the company's areas of expertise, and onboard activities for families make for an unfussy European vacation.

HURTIGRUTEN

One of the most unique cruises in the world (with two hybrid fuel/electric ships), these ships deliver mail, cargo, locals and intrepid passengers year-round to the western Norwegian coast. You'll pass the Arctic Circle, watch the Northern Lights or midnight sun and go dogsledding or ice fishing. Hurtigruten has a 'Young Explorers Programme' for kids 7 through 13, too.

Epic Cruise Experiences

Watch the Northern Lights inside the Arctic Circle. (Hurtigruten guarantees a viewing on their 12-day cruises or you get a free week-long cruise.)

—

In the summer, experience the midnight sun at North Cape, the most northerly point on the European mainland.

—

Hang on and cry, "mush!" Try your hand at dogsledding with lovable, if slightly malodorous, Siberian Huskies in Norway, Sweden, or Finland.

—

Catch the Mariinsky Ballet and the opera when you spend two or even three visa-free days in Tsar Peter the Great's grandiose St Petersburg, Russia.

—

Learn about the indigenous local Sami culture.

THE CRUISE HANDBOOK

LIFESAVER TIP
MANY MEDITERRANEAN CITIES
(INCLUDING FLORENCE, CAIRO
AND ROME) ARE AN HOUR OR MORE
INLAND FROM WHERE THE
SHIPS DOCK, SO GROUP TOURS
ARE A NECESSITY.

○ Adventure
○ Outdoors
○ Culture

MEDITERRANEAN

From Istanbul and Rome to southern France and the Spanish coast, Mediterranean cruises cover it all. Part history tour, part beach and sun vacation, part culinary odyssey, this region offers a veritable feast, whether at a world-class city or dipping into the Greek islands.

The ancient Persians, Minoans, Greeks, and Phoenicians – sailing the waters Mediterranean for trade, commerce, and conquest was a rite of passage for every civilization that rose to dominance in the Mediterranean Basin. As you tour Malta's 5300-year-old Tarxien Temples, climb up to Athens' 2500-year-old Acropolis or pretend to be a gladiator at the relatively young 2050-year-old Roman Colosseum, you can't help but feel a part of that antiquity.

Mediterranean cruises cover an astounding amount of the world's most culturally rich destinations.

Many sail from Morocco, Portugal and Spain in the west (the Atlantic's Canary Islands appear on a few itineraries); through the southern Europe juggernauts of France, Italy, Croatia and Greece; around the history-drenched islands of Corsica, Malta, Sicily and Sardinia; and on to the eastern Mediterranean countries of Turkey and Israel. Several cruise lines visit North African destinations like Egypt or Tunisia (home of the seafaring Phoenicians' Carthage). The Mediterranean Sea is relatively compact, so it's possible to cover two of these segments in one week, and all four in two weeks.

Left: Malta's fortified city of Senglea; Above: Gaudi's Sagrada Familia in Barcelona

THE CRUISE HANDBOOK

Mediterranean cruises are popular with multi-generational families, as most of the larger ships come with kids rooms and activities. Many shore excursions are well equipped for travellers with mobility limitations, which can be invaluable in difficult-to-maneuver hilltop towns and cobblestone streets. If you prefer a more informal routine, smaller ships and adventure expeditions have fewer onboard activities but stop in at more off-the-beaten-path destinations.

Prefer relaxing on a beach but travelling with someone who wants to do more sightseeing? A Mediterranean cruise offers more than exemplary historic sites, and can be perfect for travellers whose interests don't always align. There's something for everyone: beautiful natural sights with cultural highlights, pristine beaches for relaxation days and incredible food and architecture along the way. (Check out Gaudi in Barcelona before snacking at the Mercat de la Boqueria.)

With so many cruises to choose from, it's possible to choose radically different ways to see the Mediterranean. Options range from an eight-person, small-boat, adventure expedition that navigates its way around tiny islands to a luxury 60-person yacht with your own private butler, or a 4000-person floating resort complete with its own spa, casino and musical revue theatre.

The larger ocean-going vessels run by major cruise lines are tailor-made for first-timers to Europe or the Mediterranean and visit its major cities: Rome, Athens, Barcelona, Venice and Istanbul. To add a little variety, many add lesser-known ports that passengers might find equally or even more fascinating: Kotor, Montenegro; Haifa,

Below: Zakynthos Island in Greece

CARRIER OPTIONS

BLUE CRUISES

For a great deal on a short, small cruise that's popular with younger cruisers, check out Turkey's Aegean coast on a Blue Cruise. All-inclusives on gulets can be booked in Fethiye or Olympos. These traditional wooden boats function as floating hostels and will take you to incredible swimming spots as well as a pirate bar accessible by dinghy.

OVERSEAS ADVENTURE TRAVEL

With no more than 16 passengers at a time, Overseas Adventure Travel (OAT) offers small ship voyages for travellers over 50. OAT was founded by a schoolteacher interested in cultural exchanges, and it shows in the port experiences: visiting a local school, helping in a harvest or eating lunch in a local home. Their nimble boats are able to reach the smallest of cruise ports, so the itineraries are more adventurous.

WINDSTAR CRUISES

With unique itineraries and a casual but upscale atmosphere, Windstar offers both yacht-style cruising and tall-masted sailing ships for 150 to 300 passengers. The 1 to 1.5 crew-to-passenger ratio means their hospitality is some of the highest rated in the business, great for arranging activities or catering to dietary or other special needs.

HIGHLIGHT

Food on the Mediterranean is king: pesto in Genoa, artichokes alla Romana in Rome, simit and lahmacun (street-food lamb pizza) in Istanbul, souvlaki and baklava in Athens, halvah in Haifa, pasta. . . well, everywhere in Italy. Mediterranean food has been touted as one of the healthiest (and most delicious) diets in the world for a reason. Mediterranean cruises are now joining their riverboat counterparts by offering more interactive culinary excursions on shore: making ravioli in Italy, tasting cheeses in France and visiting wineries in Portugal. Most cruise lines offer an onboard Mediterranean or local menu in addition to American or international fare.

Epic Cruise Experiences

Discover firsthand the cradle of Western civilization at the Acropolis in Athens, the Parthenon in Rome, Carthage in Tunisia or Ephesus in Turkey.

—

Wend through whitewashed walls topped with blue domes on the ancient island of Santorini, where Bronze Age culture dates back to 3000 BCE.

—

Experience two of the world's Blue Zones – Sardinia and Greece – where people regularly live to be 100 years old. Could it be eating the salted fish, freshly pressed olive oil and fresh tomato sauces? Tuck in and find out.

—

Wait, we're not done with food. Truffle hunt in southern France, make pasta in Italy or tour Istanbul's spice bazaar.

THE CRUISE HANDBOOK

Israel; Split, Croatia; or Ajaccio, Corsica. Because sites are often somewhat inland, many ports are known not for their cities but for their nearby attractions, especially in Italy with Naples (Pompeii), Livorno (nearby Florence and the Leaning Tower of Pisa), and La Spezia (along the Cinque Terre coastline).

As the size of the boat goes down, the costs often go up, but so does the intimacy, adventurousness and exclusivity of the voyage. Expedition ships and luxury yachts often stick to a far more compact region: the Greek Islands, the Adriatic seaports of Croatia and Italy, or Spain and Morocco.

Above: Easter Festival in Malta; Below: Hvar Island, Croatia; Opposite: Sunrise at Little Venice on Mykonos in Greece

ISTANBUL

Enter Istanbul near the mouth of the Bosphorus and soon you see the Hagia Sophia and the Blue Mosque rising out of one of the world's grandest cities. Many cruises can arrange visits to a hammam (a Turkish bath). In an ancient stone bathhouse, an attendant scrubs away so much dirt, you'll feel reborn. The pounds may come back, however, as you sample Turkish delight or eat the world's favourite street food, doner kebab, in its home country. The Grand Bazaar with its maze of shops and booths and the Spice Bazaar showcase the Ottoman Empire's history of trade and make for unique souvenir shopping. Many ships overnight in Istanbul for two full days of sightseeing, and as you cross the Bosphorus on a local ferry while drinking a cup of Turkish tea, you may wish the trip were longer.

Itinerary

7 DAYS
One week will give you a good overview of the western Mediterranean region, as you cruise from Rome to Florence, Cannes, Majorca, Barcelona and Naples. Prefer the Adriatic and the Greek isles? Depart from Venice and head to Dubrovnik and Kotor before heading towards Greece and Santorini.

12+ DAYS
Cruises that approach the two-week-plus mark don't have to confine themselves to any one direction, but can range from Santorini and Athens to Seville and Morocco, while covering many of the major ports along the way. Smaller luxury or adventure ships often delve deep into one specific zone, whether it be the Greek Islands or the Dalmatian and Adriatic coasts.

THE CRUISE HANDBOOK

LIFESAVER TIP

iF YOU DECiDE TO PLAN YOUR
OWN EXCURSiONS ONSHORE, SET
AN ALARM ON YOUR PHONE
TO REMiND YOU TO
RETURN TO THE SHiP
ON TiME.

- Outdoors
- Beach
- Relaxation

CARiBBEAN

The Caribbean is the world's leading cruise destination, outpacing every other region in passengers. It's not hard to guess why. Nestled in a warm and sunny climate, with over 30 distinct ports, the region is rich in colonial plazas and beaches. Each of the western, eastern, or southern cruises offers a different and specialized selection of balmy delights.

Typical eastern Caribbean ports of call include San Juan, St Thomas, St Maarten and the Bahamas, while western Caribbean cruise itineraries stop at Grand Cayman, Jamaica, the Mexican Caribbean and sometimes Central American destinations like Belize and Honduras. Southern Caribbean cruises visit the French West Indies and the ABC Islands, with stops in Martinique, Guadaloupe, St Barts, St Lucia, Dominica, Grenada, Aruba, Bonaire and Curacao, potentially stopping in Cartagena, Colombia as well.

Caribbean cruises often start in Florida or Puerto Rico, but departures from New York or the Bahamas are possible, too. Trips tend to be five to seven days, but you can find longer or shorter trips by hunting for a package that suits your needs.

The western Caribbean is best distinguished by its stellar Mayan ruins and sparkly beaches. Because there's more distance to cover between ports, cruise-goers on western itineraries often enjoy more time relaxing on the boat, getting to enjoy onboard experiences and entertainment. Don't let that fool you, though. The onshore experiences are second to none, with top-notch tours of ancient Mayan ruins such as Tulum or Chichen Itza, zip-lining in the Yucatecan jungle

Left: A beach bar in Barbados; Above: Snorkeling at Grace Bay in The Turks and Caicos Islands

SAN JUAN

San Juan, Puerto Rico is a unique and vibrant city full of history and culinary delights. Tour the historic citadel Castillo San Felipe del Morro (a national historic site) with its evocative ramparts and walls and then stop in Plaza de Colon to take in the ambiance. As recovery from Hurricane Maria continues, tourist amenities have slowly returned, and the re-opened cafes and restaurants can give you a taste of the national dish, plaintain-based mofongo.

and diving on Isla Cozumel, one of the highest-rated dive sites in the world. There's also fantastic shopping at portside markets and regional cuisine as haute as anywhere else in the world. Belize offers diving and beaches that will definitely fill your memory bank, and Grand Cayman, home to the village of Hell, has perfect sandy beaches for lounging and great shopping opportunities.

In the eastern Caribbean, one stops more frequently and spends more time on shore. Shorter distances between stops means a busier schedule with less time to lounge on the deck, which can seem hectic to some, as you move from port to

WHO'S IT FOR

Caribbean cruising is ideal for just about anyone from families and honeymooners to leisure-lovers and adventurers. Take a relaxing shore excursion or a trip to tour the Mayan ruins. Sailing these Caribbean seas gets your toes wet on pink sandy beaches while experiencing a taste of West Indian culture.

Itinerary

4 DAYS

In four days, you'll make a round trip with a lone port as a destination, such as Miami–Cozumel–Miami or Galveston–Costa Maya–Galveston. A day of sailing will be followed by an overnight in Cozumel, Playa del Carmen or Costa Maya. After that it's back to port. Short but sweet.

7 DAYS

A seven-day trip could bring you from Port Canaveral to Amber Cove, St Thomas, San Juan and lastly, Grand Turk before returning to port via a final day of ocean waves and Caribbean blue.

Left, top & bottom: Aruba's seashore; San Juan's city walls; Top & above: Old San Juan; a refreshing mojito

THE CRUISE HANDBOOK

Find the sleeping giant Mount Liamuiga, a dormant volcano on St Kitts whose slopes harbour a variety of birds and wildlife.

—

Both a shopper and a Europhile? Don't miss out on the St Barts experience, where dining and shopping are chic and snazzy.

CARRIER OPTIONS

DISNEY CRUISE LINE

The Caribbean is a popular destination for families with young kids, and Disney's cruise line knows exactly how to delight its audience. Don't expect much in the way of nightlife and singles' parties, but for families who might otherwise have gone to Disney World, this will certainly provide a magical place on Earth.

CARNIVAL CRUISE LINE

Catering to first-time cruisers, this line often has many 20- and 30-somethings as passengers, along with some options for family and kids' entertainment. Expect the nightlife to be boisterous well into the wee hours on most voyages, with casinos, discos and bars open late.

PRINCESS CRUISES

This company's ship *Pacific Princess* was the star of the television series *The Love Boat* and kicked off an explosion of Caribbean cruising after its airing in 1977. Princess Cruises feature more experienced passengers, aged around 30 to 70, and a wide mix of families.

port. But this island hopping is also part of what makes eastern Caribbean cruising so fun. The ports of call are all stunning beach spots in their own right, though there is less variation in the excursions than on a western Caribbean cruise. Some of the shopping rivals what you'd find in the Mediterranean Riviera, both in its luxury and its price tag. You may not find as many deals on these excursions, but you will find interesting goods worthy of gift-giving or fun mementos to take home. You're also able to experience a lot in a relatively short amount of time, going home with great memories.

Southern Caribbean cruises give you the option to visit a few truly unique spots, such as Aruba and Curacao, as well as a chance to set foot in South America if you so desire. The desert-like landscapes of Aruba are like no other in the region, and as such make for some fascinating shore excursions that are a far-cry from typical Caribbean fare.

HIGHLIGHT

Southern Caribbean cruises stopping in Bonaire give scuba divers a luxurious taste of one of the world's best reefs. Bonaire National Marine Park has been protected since 1979 and offers incredible biodiversity. Some cruise lines, like Royal Caribbean, even offer PADI certification on board. Heading to the western Caribbean? You can find great diving off the coast of Cozumel, Mexico.

THE CRUISE HANDBOOK

LiFESAVER TiP

ALLOW A FEW DAYS TO GET OVER YOUR JET LAG BEFORE BOARDING OR YOU COULD MISS THE FIRST PART OF YOUR CRUISE DUE TO BEING OVER-TIRED.

○ Adventure
○ Outdoors
● Culture

AUSTRALIA & NEW ZEALAND

Cruising "down under" offers an easy, enjoyable and cost-effective way to experience the best of Australia and New Zealand. Cruising Australia's long travel distances is a pleasure rather than a chore and the colorful variety of ports offers travellers of all ages an irresistible mix of culture, adventure and outdoor fun.

Whether you're seeking amazing food and wine, cultural immersion, action and adventure or natural beauty, Australia and New Zealand have it all. Most cruises depart from Australia's eastern coast, with Sydney being the most popular port, and travel north up the Queensland coast or south towards New Zealand. Itineraries generally range from seven to fourteen days, with some lines offering a handful of shorter trips.

Most passengers hail from Australia and New Zealand, but there is a sprinkling of nationalities from around the world. During the Australian and New Zealand school holidays, you'll find plenty of families on board, but otherwise passenger ages are mixed. There is a ship to suit every traveller, with choices ranging from family-friendly, mainstream lines to boutique, five-star luxury ships and everything in between. Ask the locals for tips on things to see and do in port; they're unfailingly friendly and will be delighted to help.

Cruising north along Australia's east coast offers the chance to experience some of the country's most famous highlights. Snorkel the Great Barrier Reef, see kangaroos

Left: Whitehaven Beach of the Whitsunday Islands; Above: A Māori mask from Rotorua

SYDNEY

Consider spending a few days in Sydney, Australia's most popular and entertaining port, before or after your cruise. Climb the Harbour Bridge for a bird's-eye view of Sydney Harbour or take a behind-the-scenes tour of the Opera House. You don't need to be an arts buff to appreciate the beauty (and scandalous stories) associated with this iconic building. Stroll around the historic Rocks area and visit The Rocks Discovery Museum for a fascinating insight into the Sydney of old. If the weather is good, a scenic ferry ride to Manly and a swim at Manly Beach is hard to beat.

and koalas, sail around the Whitsundays or join a bush food tour led by an Indigenous guide. The choice is yours. Ports on this route such as Brisbane, Cairns and Airlie Beach are friendly, laid-back and easy to navigate

on foot. Some Queensland cruises include Fraser Island or Moreton Island, two of the world's largest sandy islands.

If you set sail from an east coast port and head south, Melbourne, with its famous laneways decorated with spectacular street art and filled with hip cafes, will almost certainly be on your itinerary and worth every moment. Newcastle has beautiful inner-city beaches and one of the country's most famous wine regions, the Hunter Valley, is located just 45 minutes away by car. Visitors to Hobart who venture beyond the historic waterfront are rewarded with cutting edge contemporary art at the world-famous MONA gallery and the intriguing, penal-colony history of Port Arthur.

Speaking of Hobart, if your cruise visits Tasmania, you will

Above: Sydney Harbour has a lively outdoor nightlife scene

need to cross Bass Strait. Bass Strait doesn't look like much on the map but this stretch of water separating Tasmania from mainland Australia is renowned for its impressively large waves. The Tasman, which separates Australia and New Zealand, shares a similar reputation. Sometimes the trip can be as smooth as silk, but more often than not, it's a wild ride. Provided you come prepared with seasickness medication, you should be fine.

With easy-to-access ports and stunning scenery, New Zealand has more than its fair share of "don't miss" natural wonders – surely a reason that the country sees 400,000 cruise visitors each year, according to Venture

CARRIER OPTIONS

CELEBRITY CRUISES

Celebrity Cruises has Australia and New Zealand's highest-rated cruise ship, *Celebrity Solstice*, which offers a contemporary and affordable take on modern luxury with some of the best suites at sea. Relaxed yet exceptional service, impressive dining options and a first-rate children's program give this line wide-ranging appeal.

CORAL EXPEDITIONS

With a fleet of ships carrying less than 80 passengers, Coral Expeditions offers a boutique cruise experience for adventurous travellers who like to explore isolated gems. Take note solo travellers: Great Barrier Reef cruises are single-supplement free year-round. Other destinations include Tasmania and the Kimberley's remote wilderness and coastline.

ROYAL CARIBBEAN

Young-at-heart travellers and families, particularly those with tweens and teens, will enjoy exploring Australia and New Zealand with Royal Caribbean. High-energy activities such as surfing on the FlowRider surf simulator, ice skating, bumper cars and skydiving at sea ensure there is never a dull moment on these ships.

HIGHLIGHT

Natural wonders are everywhere when cruising in Australia and New Zealand. Snorkel among jewel-bright fish on the Great Barrier Reef or take a walk through Australia's World Heritage-listed Daintree Rainforest. Near Port Douglas you will find Mossman Gorge, the oldest, continuously surviving rainforest on earth. In New Zealand you can swim with wild Hector's dolphins in Akaroa or see boiling mud in Rotorua. Soak up the sun on the pristine white sands of Whitehaven Beach or cool off in a waterhole outside Darwin at Litchfield National Park. The mighty waterfalls, misty fjords, lush rainforest and towering granite peaks of New Zealand's Fiordland are beautiful, rain, hail or shine.

Epic Cruise Experiences

Go snorkeling or learn to dive on the Great Barrier Reef.

—

Take an Art Deco walking tour in Napier, home to one of the largest and best preserved collections of this type of architecture in the world.

—

See koalas, kangaroos and other native animals at an Australian wildlife park.

—

Paddle a waka (canoe) with your fellow shipmates and a Māori guide who shares personal, tribal and family stories during the journey.

—

Sample fine wines and enjoy the scenery at Hawke's Bay in New Zealand or Australia's picturesque Hunter Valley or Yarra Valley wine regions.

THE CRUISE HANDBOOK

Southland. French-influenced Akaroa's picturesque harbour is home to over 15,000 Hector's dolphins, the rarest oceanic dolphin in the world. Stunning scenery abounds at Dusky Sound, Doubtful Sound and Milford Sound, all of which can be seen in one day on a cruise ship.

Tauranga is the gateway to Rotorua, one of the best spots in New Zealand to experience Māori culture and the country's famous geysers, boiling mud and thermal activity. It's also the place to scare yourself silly with excursions involving things like a luge ride or plummeting down the world's highest commercially rafted waterfall. If you fancy a drink to steady your nerves after all that excitement, you're in luck. New Zealand's craggy mountains and stunning rural scenery provide the perfect backdrop for wine tasting at the country's many stellar wineries.

WHO'S iT FOR

Australia and New Zealand offer something for everyone from families, adventurers and nature lovers to mature travellers, sun-worshippers and food and wine fanatics. Visitors rave about how friendly Australians and New Zealanders are, and it's impossible not to be captivated by the enthusiasm, warmth and humor of those who live in this part of the world. While Australia and New Zealand have some truly amazing sights, it's the friendly encounters that are most likely to stay with you. And for Oceania natives, cruises offer a chance to experience old sights anew.

Itinerary

7 DAYS

For a short and sweet experience, take a seven-night cruise up the Queensland coast with a stop at the Whitsundays and a trip to beautiful Whitehaven Beach. Nearby Cairns is famous for being the gateway to the Great Barrier Reef while Port Douglas offers the chance to connect with the local Kuku Yalanji people on an interpretive walk led by an Indigenous guide.

14 DAYS

Stay a little longer by spending 14 nights on a trip departing from Australia or Auckland and explore the natural beauty, thriving cultural scene and Māori heritage of New Zealand. Take a guided tour with a Māori guide at Te Papa, New Zealand's national museum, see albatrosses, visit a historic brewery in Dunedin or sail an America's Cup yacht in Auckland's Waitemata Harbour.

THE CRUISE HANDBOOK

LIFESAVER TIP

LEARN A LITTLE ABOUT
DIGITAL PHOTOGRAPHY BEFORE
YOU GO, AS YOU WON'T
BE ABLE TO STOP
TAKING PHOTOS OF THE
AMAZING VIEWS.

Practicalities

💼 Layers are paramount! Pack long underwear, a flexible, lightweight insulation layer, a waterproof and windproof outer layer, a hooded parka and calf-length, flexible waterproof boots with heavy socks and sock liners. Don't forget your hat, gloves and neck gaiter for particularly chilly days.

🚢 Ushuaia, Argentina; Punta Arenas, Chile; Invercargill, New Zealand

📅 Travel is only possible during the Antarctic summer from November to March. Peak season, with the most daylight, is mid-December through January.

$ $ $ $

○ Adventure
○ Outdoors

ANTARCTICA

The Antarctic is a naturalist's dream. Untouched by humans, visitors can truly disconnect from civilisation as they experience an environment sculpted by nature's powerful forces. Whales, penguins and seals live happily in the shadow of craggy peaks while magnificent icebergs drift through glassy waters.

A trip to Antarctica is an adventure into wilderness. Giant icebergs split and echo from enormous ice shelves. Adult penguins slide into the ocean to fish for their chicks waiting on shore. Whales cut through frigid waters, launching themselves into the air in pure celebration. Leopard seals float atop icebergs, waiting for a snack to cross their path. Antarctica is truly nature at her finest.

Every trip to Antarctica will reveal something new and unexpected, with each route offering varied glimpses into the land of ice and snow. Along the route leaving from South America, ships transit through the otherworldly Drake Passage to encounter stunning scenery and environments teeming with wildlife. The classic eleven-day Peninsula cruises stop in the South Shetland Islands to check out the Adélie and chinstrap penguin colonies as well as the Antarctic fur seals and southern elephant seals who rule the beaches.

The ships then proceed to navigate through the towering rock faces and spectacular glaciers of the Gerlache Strait, the Neumayer Channel and the Lemaire Channel to land on the continent proper at aptly-named Paradise Bay. This is the most accessible part of Antarctica,

Left: Adventure cruising in Antarctica; Above: A young emperor penguin

HIGHLIGHT

~~~~~~~~~~

Escape into a pristine world of blue-white ice glistening in the summer sun. Marvel at the rocky peaks stretching to the sky and reflected in the perfectly glassy surface of the ocean below. Listen to sounds of penguins singing, ice calving and whales surfacing.

extending up towards Patagonia and requiring only three days at sea to reach.

For the more adventurous traveller, a 12- to 14-day expedition across the Antarctic Circle (at latitude 66°33' south) approaches the heart of the continent. Initial passes of the South Shetland Islands bring in all the biodiversity of a classic peninsula trip, and if the weather allows crossing the Antarctic Circle, it provides the once-in-a-lifetime sight of perpetual daylight over stunningly odd ice formations.

Above: Icebergs in the Yalour Islands; Right: Paradise Bay

If you have even more time (19 to 25 days), a voyage that includes the Falkland Islands and South Georgia Island is a worthwhile itinerary. Boats first stop in the Falkland Islands to view the colonies of rockhopper and Magellanic penguins.

They also carry on to Stanley, where one can learn about its fascinating history, meet hearty locals and explore its shops and pubs. Accessible only by boat, South Georgia Island is home to

CARRIER OPTIONS

ONE OCEAN EXPEDITIONS

For an expedition ship easier on the budget, try the sister ships *Akademik Vavilov* and *Akademik Ioffe*. These twin Scandinavian-built, Russian research vessels offer a plethora of itinerary choices with modest accommodations. With a maximum capacity of 92 and plenty of adventure add-ons, a journey on one of these vessels can take you exactly where you'd like to go.

PONANT

This French luxury expedition line has regularly introduced new, top-of-the-line ships with some even on the cutting edge of being emissions-free (as well as being on the cutting edge of cutting through ice).

ABERCROMBIE & KENT

This tour operator specializing in luxury expedition ships has all-inclusive sailings that showcase an above-average roster of lecturers. They also offer a family-focused cruise over the December holidays and can provide cruisetours to extend your trip.

Camp in Antarctica and experience its wonderful deep silence, broken only by the calls of penguins or the crack of ice in the distance.

—

Paddle around glittering mega-icebergs on a kayak, or paddleboard as whales glide underneath the waters.

—

Explore the 10,000-foot peaks that jut from the ocean deep, by cross-country ski or snowshoe.

—

Have the expert photographer on board teach you how to capture that perfect photo of a penguin chick finding his sea legs.

—

Pay homage to Shackleton with a whisky toast at his grave, located in Grytviken, South Georgia.

THE CRUISE HANDBOOK

WHO'S IT FOR

Adventurers who long to fling themselves to the furthest corners of the world should all have Antarctica on their bucket list. Meanwhile, wildlife-enthusiasts devoted to seeking out the most intimate animal encounters will forever remember the day a whale swam past their zodiac, or the time a curious adolescent penguin pecked at their boots. High price tags mean that this isn't a trip to be taken lightly, but last-minute deals are possible (yet still likely to cost at least US$3500).

Key
Port
Feature

the largest colony of the mighty king penguin as well as the nesting albatross. In Salisbury Plain, tens of thousands of king penguins nest in the tussac grass, singing loudly to each other and curiously greeting newcomers from the ship. Elephant and fur seals lounge on the beach and southern giant petrels hunt from above.

For history buffs, South Georgia Island is also notable as the last leg of Sir Ernest Shackleton's famous journey on the *Endurance* and the site of his grave. To stop over here is to follow in the footsteps of one of the greatest explorers in modern history. Some expeditions may also include the Weddell Sea, a rarely visited, beautiful region home to the Snow Hill Island emperor penguin.

If coming to the Antarctic from Australia or New Zealand, cruises spend longer at sea to reach the continent but are able to experience the Ross Sea region, including Mt Erebus, the

southernmost active volcano in the world.

For all Antarctic cruises, remember the weather conditions determine landings and wildlife sightings. Try to choose a specialised ship with a helicopter on board for finding seabird rookeries and giving everyone a chance to observe these elusive birds. Naturalists and expedition leaders on board are well equipped to answer any questions about this seldom-visited region.

USHUAIA

Ushuaia, Argentina is a common embarkation point sitting below the snow-capped Martial range where the Andes meet the Beagle Channel. If you've forgotten anything for your journey, you can find it here. There is also a plethora of hiking, sailing, skiing and kayaking opportunities. The beer scene around the world's southernmost microbrews isn't bad either.

PUNTA ARENAS

A bit of a sprawling metropolis despite its bottom-of-the-world status, urban sprawl on the Strait of Magellan makes easy connections to Tierra del Fuego, Torres del Paine as well as Antarctica. King crab is a local delicacy.

Left: Icebergs in Pleneau Bay;
Right: A summer night near the pole

Itinerary

8 DAYS
Since Antarctica is so far from anywhere that getting there and back takes time. After two days on the Drake Passage, a typical Antarctic Peninsula trip gives you four days to island hop and explore the colonies of the adelie, chinstrap and gentoo penguins. You'll cruise through the pristine wilderness of snow, and ice with a chance of seeing minke, orca and humpback whales as well as Weddell, crabeater and leopard seals.

23 DAYS
With a little more than three weeks, you'll sail through the South Georgia and Falkland Islands, giving you a more complete and varied experience of the region. After a day of sailing, greet the Falkland Islands where you can learn its fascinating history and have tea in one of the charming villages. Then it's off to South Georgia Island where the soaring, snow-clad mountains and massive glaciers host huge king penguin rookeries and thousands of sub-Antarctic fur seals – all before reaching the Antarctic Peninsula.

THE CRUISE HANDBOOK

LiFESAVER TiP

THiS PART OF THE WORLD CAN BE A DOOZY WHEN iT COMES TO STOMACH AND OTHER iLLNESSES. BE PREPARED WiTH ANTiBiOTiCS AND MEDiCATiONS TO GET YOU BACK OUT SiGHTSEEiNG.

AFRiCA & EGYPT

Africa is an entire world unto itself. Colourful and chaotic, breathtaking and humbling, its range of experiences span from intimate wild animal encounters to stunning beaches and buzzing urban areas. Not for the faint of heart, but for those with a bit more of an adventurous soul, this melting pot of cultures, cuisines, religions and history is guaranteed to amaze.

Practicalities

🚢 Alexandria and Luxor, Egypt; Tunis, Tunisia; Algiers, Algeria; Casablanca, Morocco; Cape Town, South Africa

💼 Long and light is the way to go: long sleeves, long pants/skirts in a light fabric to protect from the sun and bugs but stay airy.

📅 Avoid Northern Africa in summer and remember that South African seasons are the reverse of those in the Northern Hemisphere.

$ $ $

⦿ Adventure
◯ Outdoors
⦿ Culture

Cruises in Africa cover a wide gamut, from luxury trips down the Nile to wildlife spotting on the Chobe River and conventional cruising out of South Africa. For ancient-history buffs, a cruise along Egypt's Nile river is an absolute-must, bucket-list item. These cruises are often coupled together with a cruisetour of Cairo and the Pyramids of Giza and ultimately provide the opportunity to see some of the most important ancient Egyptian relics such as Luxor, the Temple of Karnak, the Valley of the Kings, the Temple of Kom Ombo and Philae Temple. While the itineraries are culture and touring intensive, there are opportunities to relax by the small but adequate pools that most river-cruise ships on the Nile feature on their sundecks – just chill while watching the palm-flanked banks float by. Most cruises end in Aswan, an oasis-like retreat that is the ideal place to wind down after a Nile cruise.

For those who are intrigued by the beauty and mystery of the Sahara Desert, a Mediterranean cruise that incorporates North Africa is sure to be of interest. Here, at the crossroads of Europe, Africa and the Arab world, travellers will experience a vibrant mix of cultures, architectural styles and cuisines – all where the

THE CRUISE HANDBOOK ▶

Above: Elephants bathing; Below: Cape Town from above

desert literally meets the sea. The intermingling of religions plays a strong role in this part of Africa, where the dominant religion is Islam, as evident in its influence on monuments such as the Hassan II Mosque in Casablanca and the Roman Catholic Notre Dame d'Afrique basilica in Algiers.

Egypt's Alexandria serves as a gateway to visiting the Pyramids of Giza for Mediterranean cruise passengers but has its own unique history to offer, and Tunis has more of a seaside resort feel than some of the other North African ports.

At the complete opposite end of the continent in southern Africa, the destinations have a markedly different feel. Safari lovers, looking for the comfort and convenience of a cruise experience, might opt for a Chobe River cruise in Namibia and Botswana where passengers will be looking for hippo and elephant sightings along the water. From these cruises a full-day safari in Chobe National Park is often provided, where travellers will be searching for elephants, giraffes, zebras, lions and cheetahs, among other wildlife. These shorter three- or four-day river cruises are typically combined with a much more comprehensive land itinerary that includes a visit

ABERCROMBIE & KENT

On the Nile, four Abercrombie & Kent vessels offer a traditional 12-passenger sailboat and 80-passenger river cruise ship with luxury amenities.

OBEROI LUXURY NILE CRUISERS AND MOVENPICK

The 54-passenger *Oberoi Zahra* and 44-passenger *Oberoi Philae* offer luxury for less and include some sprawling suites, spa facilities and a pool deck but aren't well suited for families with young children. For a greater variety of options, Swiss company Movenpick has eight Nile ships from basic to upscale.

OCEANIA CRUISES

Luxury Oceania has yearly two-week or month-long African coast cruises on the *Nautica*, often starting or ending in Cape Town before touring a rich variety of destinations from Kenya and Cote d'Ivoire to Madagascar and Senegal.

CROISIEUROPE

For a cruise-safari along the Chobe River, the more accessibly priced French company, CroisiEurope, offers a chance to spy wildlife from the deck of the *African Dream*, and itineraries often include extensive overland tours.

HIGHLIGHT

The food in Africa is as diverse as its people, with a long history of melding cultures and spices. From Egyptian food incorporating small plates such as ful, a popular fava bean dip, and ta'meya (Egyptian falafel), to Moroccan dishes like tagine stews and couscous, to the Indian influence in south and east African curry dishes, variety rules the roost. There is plenty of meat (typically grilled or in a curry or stew) in African cuisine, but it's quite easy to find local vegan and vegetarian options.

Epic Cruise Experiences

Take an excursion to Fez to see a North African city frozen in time.

—

Visit the UNESCO-ranked Medina on a cruisetour for a glimpse of the medieval university city.

—

See the soaring statues of Abu Simbel in Egypt. You might think you've had it with ancient Egyptian temples, but these may very well top everything else you've seen before.

—

Take a wildlife safari in South Africa's Kruger National Park, or visit the Masai Mara in Kenya or the Serengeti in Tanzania. These will make your Africa cruise experience that much more memorable, even if just for a day or two.

—

Arrange a cruisetour to see one of the natural wonders of the world – Victoria Falls.

to the stunning Victoria Falls in Zambia/Zimbabwe, and possibly South Africa.

South Africa itself serves as the anchor for several Atlantic and Indian Ocean cruises that sail along the southern tip of the continent, stopping in places like the beautiful and lively Cape Town with its trademark scenic overlook, Table Mountain. Further east, South Africa's Port Elizabeth and Durban are beach cities with unique vibes all their own – Durban is more of a big city, while Port Elizabeth is popular with tourists. For hardcore beach lovers, you may want to invest in a cruise that heads all the way to the Seychelles. Here the pristine beaches and turquoise blue waters are among some of the most beautiful in the world.

Left: A dhow off the Kenyan coast; Below: Bushbuck on the Chobe River; Right: Nelson Mandela banner on Robben Island Prison

Key Port Feature

CAPE TOWN
Many southern Africa cruises kick off from Cape Town. Tack on a few days beforehand to explore this gorgeous coastal city. An arduous hike or a much easier gondola ride to the top of Table Mountain is a must for the epic views.

Robben Island, which famously houses the prison where Nelson Mandela was held, is a difficult visit but a necessary one. For a truly unique accommodation, check out the Airstream trailers that flank the rooftop of the Grand Daddy hotel in Cape Town. For one of the city's most luxurious and classic properties, stay (or at least grab afternoon tea or a cocktail) at Cape Grace.

CAIRO
Any cruise along the Nile typically starts with a few days in Egypt's swarming capital. After the Pyramids of Giza and the Sphinx, make time for the Egyptian Museum in Tahrir Square and the Khan el-Khalili bazaar in historic Cairo.

ESTABLISHMENT OF ROBBEN ISLAND MUSEUM: Nelson Mandela at the launch of the Robben Island Museum in 1997. In the background are sketches of other South African anti-apartheid leaders, Govan Mbeki, Mandela, Steve Biko, Robert Sobukwe and Walter Sisulu.

Itinerary

10 DAYS

When it comes to Egypt, you can't go wrong with the classic Nile itinerary. In 10 days you will visit Cairo, the Pyramids and all the quintessential ancient Egyptian sites along the Nile at a pace befitting antiquity.

24 DAYS

Hop on a Western Africa cruise down the coast from Lisbon to Cape Town, visiting places not many tourists go while cruising in style. This is bound to be a cruise and journey of a lifetime. Carrier options are fewer than for regions such as the Caribbean and Mediterranean, but a select number of lines offer trips along the coast of Africa each year that are worth seeking out.

WHO'S iT FOR

Africa is great for anyone from honeymooners to retirees as long as they are hardy travellers and interested in experiencing vastly different cultures. The itineraries tend to be culture heavy, but depending on the sailing there is often at least a little time built in for some relaxation and recuperation.

LIFESAVER TIP
TO ENRICH YOUR EXPERIENCE, PICK ONE HIGHLIGHT ALONG YOUR ROUTE – SUCH AS REMBRANDT AND THE DUTCH GOLDEN AGE OR ROMAN HISTORY – AND STUDY UP BEFORE YOU CRUISE.

Practicalities

Cologne, Germany; Paris, France; Amsterdam, Netherlands; Basel, Switzerland; Kiev, Ukraine

Riverboat cabins are usually smaller than ocean-going vessels, so pack light with resort-casual layers and (very) comfortable walking shoes.

Starting in April and running through the Christmas market season, European river cruise popularity peaks in July, August and September.

$ $ $ $

- Adventure
- Outdoors
- Culture

EUROPEAN RiVER CRUiSES

Sip your syrah while watching a full slate of European scenery breeze past – castles, medieval villages and fields of flowers. European river cruises are elegantly casual affairs, perfect for exploring the arts and culture that beckon ashore.

The days when European river cruising was known as a stuffy, stodgy affair are over. Active travellers, nature and culture aficionados and families of all sizes have discovered that cruising down a quiet, traffic-free river, surrounded by scenic riverfront views, is an ideal way to see Europe. This change in European travel is unfolding in real time, as each year more and more cruise lines offer immersive learning experiences like cooking classes and home visits, or activities like bicycle trips and long hikes.

The two major rivers for European cruises are the Rhine and the Danube. Together, they were once the northern boundary of the Roman Empire. Rhine cruises often run from Amsterdam to Basel, following the course of the river through Germany. Danube cruises start in southern Germany, wend their way through Slovakia, Austria, and Serbia before skirting the Bulgarian and Romanian border to reach the Black Sea.

Yet while many first-time European river cruisers stick to these two rivers, there are many other options available. Whatever your choice, a river cruise is often the best way to see destinations for the first time. In Western Europe you can cruise through the French countryside

Left: The canals in Amsterdam; **Above:** Lounging on the Seine

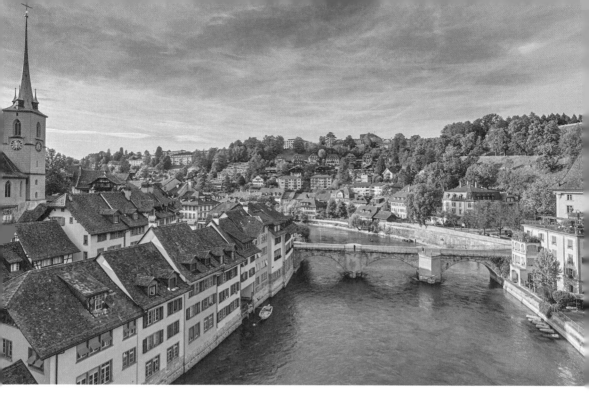

on the Moselle, Rhône and Seine, or check out the vineyards of Portugal on the Duoro. Beyond the Danube in Eastern Europe, riverboats visit the remnants of Tsarist Russia on the Volga, while in Ukraine you can cruise along the Dnieper River to the seaport of Odessa with its statuesque opera house and famed Potemkin Stairs.

Then, of course, there's the food. Many cruise lines offer a regional menu or serve almost solely local cuisine. They know guests are there to indulge and

Above: The Aare River in Bern, Switzerland; Right: Bicycling in France

therefore cook accordingly. Look for cruises where the chef offers cooking classes as an added bonus. A select few – especially in France and Portugal – even come with their own onboard sommelier.

By necessity European riverboats are far smaller than the vessels that cruise the Mediterranean or Baltic. Passengers number fewer than 190 (sometimes fewer than 20) instead of thousands. River cruises are not really geared towards very young children (and several even ban them), but many lines now have kid-friendly activities for kids ages

WHO'S iT FOR

Historically, European river cruises have attracted mostly active seniors, but today more and more are catering to multigenerational families, honeymooners and even young solo travellers. A few cruise lines – including CroisiEurope, Tauck and Disney – run designated family-friendly cruises with fast-paced itineraries that teach kids totally non-boring history lessons. For the liveliest boatmates, look for an "active" cruise that comes with bicycles, adventure sports or interactive cultural experiences.

HIGHLIGHT

Many European river cruises have their own fleet of passenger bicycles. Take one out for a bike trip in the French countryside during a stop on your cruise down the Seine.

CARRIER OPTIONS

U BY UNIWORLD

U by Uniworld offers two boutique-hotel style cruise ships for passengers aged 21 to 45 (no exceptions). Think rooftop bars with yoga in the morning and DJs spinning EDM by night. Dining is farm-to-table chic and triples and solo-share options make pricing quite manageable.

GRAND CIRCLE CRUISE LINE

These are some of the most interactive cruises out there. Each day offers immersive experiences and cultural activities. Learn to make traditional German Christmas Stollen or participate in a cultural exchange with Romani women in Serbia or local students in Croatia. Every single Grand Circle Cruise offers a home visit, often including a locally cooked meal. The line caters to guests 50 and over, but all ages are welcome.

FRENCH COUNTRY WATERWAYS

Want to feel you've just stepped onto a vicomte's private vessel? French Country Waterways' luxury-hotel barges are intimate affairs with only eight to eighteen guests. Days begin with homemade croissants followed by a bike ride or a stroll through medieval villages, with wine awaiting you on your return.

Epic Cruise Experiences

Warm up with mulled wine while shopping for Christmas gifts at a Christkindlmarkt in Germany, Austria or Switzerland.

—

Pedal away from port on any number of the active cruise lines that carry an army of bicycles.

—

Sign up for an immersive shore experience: dance the waltz in Vienna, paint matroyshka dolls in St Petersburg or taste cheeses on a French farm.

—

For families, go on a scavenger hunt through Paris' Louvre museum, practice sword fighting or taste local soft drinks with your own soda sommelier.

—

See the castles, chateaus or cathedrals in virtually every port.

six and up. On board they may only have a small playroom, but kids will forgive you when they realise how much freedom they have to explore on shore each day. Enrichment programs and informative lectures for adults are the dominant onboard entertainment, with a huge range of excursion opportunities offshore. Additionally, there are no inside cabins on a European river cruise. Cabins come with a large window at the very least, and a great many have their own balcony or floor-to-ceiling panoramic view. You may even forego the ship's entertainment just to watch the scenery breeze past.

Key Port Feature

COLOGNE

Cologne, Germany dates back to Roman times. Filled with 2000 years of history, it's no surprise that there are over two dozen museums to keep you busy when you're not strolling along the pedestrianised riverfront or sipping German wines and beers in cafes. At Cologne's Roman-Germanic Museum, there is an in situ Roman mosaic, as well as the world's largest collection of Roman glass. You can also climb the tower in the Kölner Dom, Cologne's gothic cathedral with its famed spires for an incredible view. Many boats board or leave from Cologne, so book an extra day or two in town to take in all the sights.

Left: Houseboats in Amsterdam; Right: The Chain Bridge in Budapest along the Danube

Itinerary

5 DAYS

Cruise along the Moselle River and be romanced by wine festivals, medieval castles, half-timbered houses and incredible food. You can combine it with a cruise down the Rhine for a longer itinerary, but this shorter dedicated cruise will let you experience an amazing region in depth.

13 DAYS

A Moscow to St Petersburg cruise on the Volga River not only allows you to take in the two crown-jewel cities of Russia, but also stops in smaller, more historic towns, offering a slice of Russian life in the countryside that provides a counterbalance to these grand urban centers.

THE CRUISE HANDBOOK

ASIAN RIVER CRUISES

Cruising in Asia means a dizzying array of intriguing options. The biggest bucket-list items in the region are short cruises of Vietnam's Ha Long Bay – with sapphire waters and sandcastle-like karst islands – and Yangtze River cruises past ancient gorges, flooded villages and the world's biggest dam. For a slower pace, try a houseboat in the backwaters of Kerala, India or boating the Irrawaddy River in Myanmar.

○ Outdoors
◉ Culture
○ Relaxation
◉ Adventure

Left: One of Ha Long Bay's striking karsts

Depending on where in Asia you embark, your cruise experience could be anything from an overnight stay on a reconstructed teak junk (a type of Chinese ship) to a week on a luxury liner. Ha Long Bay is the spot for junk trips; in high season the water is full of wooden boats topped with gold and red sails. You can also journey down the sultry Mekong in a creaky *sampan* (flat-bottomed wooden boat) or sail the Irrawaddy on a yacht fit for a sultan. In China, cruise the Yangtze on a garishly outfitted ship complete with a tiki-themed bar. Or take a respite from the fast-paced destinations in India on a Kerala houseboat.

What these trips have in common is the extravagant natural beauty outside your port window. Spend an entire afternoon on the top deck, just goggling at the splendor. In Ha Long Bay you'll find jagged limestone islands rising from the water, their pinnacles topped with luxuriant stretches of rainforest. On the Yangtze, you'll drift through gorges carved by eons of rushing water alongside a patchwork of farming valleys and tiny villages perched like birds' nests on the mountainsides. The

rivers of Southeast Asia will offer you views of jungle-swathed riverbanks and flooded rice paddies glittering like diamonds.

There's plenty of man-made culture to be experienced along the way, too. Irrawaddy cruises travel between the ancient spiritual center of Mandalay to the plains of Bagan, with its temples as far as the eye can see, stopping at cave shrines and local villages. Yangtze cruises generally offer one or two daily shore excursions into ancient villages or pagoda temples on the riverbanks. But the true highlight of the Yangtze trip is when your ship passes through the vast

locks of the Three Gorges Dam, the largest in the world and an engineering marvel to behold.

Onboard entertainment on the larger, higher-end boats include traditional cruise activities: swimming pools, spa massages and cabaret shows. On Yangtze ships you can try an acupuncture session or listen to a lecture about jade jewelry. On smaller junks or *sampans*, fun means reading the novel you brought or playing cards with new friends.

River cruising in Southeast Asia, whether Ha Long Bay or along the Mekong, means rubbing shoulders with plenty of other foreigners, from backpackers in

Above: At the market in Ciqikou Ancient Town

Beer lao T-shirts to vacationing families with teens in tow. Some of the budget cruises have a distinct party vibe with plenty of Singha beer and cannonballs from the roof deck. In China your fellow passengers will be mostly domestic travellers, and only midrange and higher-end cruises have English-speaking staff. Take the chance to practice your karaoke skills, which translate no matter what language you speak.

Wherever you are, expect a mix of local and Western-style buffet food on board. On most cruises, this sadly leaves

CENTURY CRUISES

This midrange Yangtze option has comfy, if not opulent rooms, English-speaking staff, and entertainment such as movie nights and lectures on traditional Chinese medicine. Stops include an ancient "ghost city" and lovely scenic gorges.

BELMOND

Travel the Irrawaddy in opulence on the *Belmond Road to Mandalay*. Expect a deck-top pool, gourmet pan-Asian food, afternoon teas and a chic cocktail lounge. Itineraries range from three days to nearly two weeks with Bagan as the highlight.

CARRIER OPTIONS

PANDAW RIVER CRUISE

Visit wonder of the world Angkor Wat via a Pandaw trip from Saigon to Siem Reap. Explore floating markets, visit the Mekong river dolphins and discover the Cambodian capital of Phnom Penh, all from your teak and brass stateroom on a seven-day trip.

VEGA TRAVEL

These small affordable one- to two-day cruises on Chinese-style junks within Ha Long Bay pick you up from Hanoi in the early morning. Journeys include a kayak excursion and a beach trip. Private rooms are tidy.

HIGHLIGHT

Seize the opportunity to get up close to Ha Long Bay's natural splendour with a kayak trip. Some junk cruises offer these as a passenger excursion, or you can organise a day trip. Paddle around the craggy islands, passing traditional Vietnamese houseboats and looking for fish in the deep blue water. If kayaking's not your thing, check out some of the area's spectacular caves, with stalactites like giant shark's teeth, all illuminated with colour-changing disco lights. Or spend a day on Cat Ba Island, the bay's largest, trekking the jungle-shrouded mountains and exploring minority villages.

Epic Cruise Experiences

Be ushered into the land of the giants as you pass through the gargantuan locks of the Three Rivers Gorge of the Yangtze, as metal gates, hundreds of feet high, swing open in the dead of night.

—

Relax in a rooftop deck lounger with a sweet local coffee in hand and take in a moment of bliss as the sun sets over the karst islands of Ha Long Bay.

—

Visit Kampong Luong, a floating village on Cambodia's Tonle Sap Lake that connects to the Mekong, and discover a world of colourful wooden houses famous for its handmade pottery.

—

Eat fresh fish caught in the picturesque Chinese fishing nets of Kerala state on your houseboat cruise.

WHO'S iT FOR

Families with kids find midrange Yangtze cruises accommodating to their needs. Budget travellers dig the cultural experience of local Chinese boats, where foreigners are rare. Young backpackers booze it up on Ha Long Bay budget boats, with higher-end options on offer too. Honeymooners and retirees love the opulent privacy of riverboats on the Irrawaddy and Mekong and houseboats in Kerala, while the adventurous take local *sampans*. Want a more standard trip? Princess, Norwegian, Celebrity, Oceania, Holland America et al. sail coastal Asia with cruisetours to sights like the Great Wall.

something to be desired for more exploratory travellers. Take onshore excursions as an opportunity to experience local culinary specialties: Thai river fish grilled in banana leaves and served with spicy-sour dipping sauce, steaming bowls of Vietnamese pho from roadside stalls and sweat-inducing Chongqing hotpot.

Below: Travelling on the Irrawaddy; the temples of Bagan; Right: A floating village in Ha Long Bay

CHONGQING

The mega-metropolis of Chongqing isn't much of a tourist hot spot, but for those interested in China's history – and its future – it's a fascinating place. Explore the winding Ming Dynasty alleyways of the restored Ciqikou Ancient Town, nibbling on snacks like candied haw apples. Ride the cable car across the muddy Yangtze. Shop for luxury sunglasses in the towering glass high-rise malls of the new downtown. And absolutely, positively, eat hotpot, the city's most famous culinary offering. Chongqing was once part of Sichuan, and it shares the province's obsession with fiery chilis and mouth-numbing peppercorns. Fragrant hotpots knock your socks off with their heat, the perfect counter to the city's often-steamy weather.

Itinerary

2 DAYS

If you've only got a weekend, try a quick Ha Long Bay "two-day," which really means about 24 hours on the boat. You'll leave Hanoi in a minibus around dawn, transfer to the boat at lunchtime, and enjoy an afternoon of cruising and kayaking. The next day might bring a beach outing, and then you head to land for the transfer back to Hanoi in time for dinner.

7 DAYS

If you've got time to spare, follow the Yangtze all the way from Chongqing to Shanghai, which takes a week to 10 days (most Yangtze cruises go less than half this distance). You'll pass Ming Dynasty villages, enormous modern cities like Wuhan and mountain scenery that's inspired painters for millennia.

THE CRUISE HANDBOOK

LIFESAVER TIP
PRONE TO SEASICKNESS? CALMER WATERS (ESPECIALLY ON THE COLUMBIA RIVER) MEANS EVEN THOSE WITH MOTION SICKNESS CAN ENJOY A CRUISE.

NORTH AMERICAN RIVER CRUISES

Do scenery and relaxation sound more appealing than nightclubs and beaches? On a North American riverboat cruise, you can mosey down the Mississippi on a paddle wheel steamboat and discover the fjords on the St Lawrence River in Canada. You can even kayak and wine-taste your way through the waterfalls and gorges of the Columbia River in the Pacific Northwest.

Practicalities

🚢 Memphis, Tennessee; New Orleans, Louisiana; Portland, Oregon; Montreal, Quebec

💼 Bring comfortable layers for day and upscale, resort-casual attire for evening. Be prepared for cool breezes (or hearty winds) with a sturdy fleece and rain jacket.

📅 Cruise the lower end of the Mississippi year round, and the upper part July through October. The Columbia River is best travelled from February to early December, and May through October is perfect for cruising along the St Lawrence.

$ $ $

○ Adventure
○ Outdoors
○ Culture

river-and-canal Seaway and the Columbia River.

Except for oceangoing vessels on the St Lawrence Seaway, most American riverboat cruises have just a few hundred passengers, if that. While ocean ships are known for mixing up their active and leisurely activities on board, riverboats have a steady but gentle pace. Most ships visit a new port almost every day of their one- or two-week long trips, often for a full day and evening; you can pick the level of activity you prefer. Stroll around historic railroad museums or apple orchards, whitewater raft the Columbia River or simply relax on your balcony watching fjords or fall foliage sail by.

Worried you may be bored? Don't fret. There's almost always a historian or naturalist aboard, and sometimes several, to offer lectures and informational walking tours that deepen your understanding of the nature and culture of the surrounding area. Food has become one of the

Since the first European settlers arrived in North America, cities and towns sprang to life around its rivers and waterways. Today North America's three main navigable rivers and waterways for cruising are the Mississippi River (plus its tributaries, the Tennessee and Ohio rivers), the St Lawrence

Left: The Columbia River Gorge; Above: The mighty St Louis arch; New Orleans' moody cemeteries

top-rated activities on today's cruise lines, however river cruises take this a step further by serving local or traditional cuisine native to the region. Additionally, with no days "at sea" like traditional cruises, there is an ever-changing display of landscape for your viewing pleasure.

The Mississippi River is divided into three distinct cruise regions, each taking an entire week to traverse. The upper Mississippi from St Paul to St Louis is Mark Twain country, where paddleboats wend their way through the American heartland, past historic Native American sites and grand mansions, while keeping an eye out for bald eagles, otters or some of the most colourful fall foliage on the continent. The lower Mississippi – Memphis to New Orleans – is all about music, local cuisine and Civil War history. The middle Mississippi – from St Louis to

From top: Quebec's monumental Fairmont Le Chateau Frontenac; whale watching from on deck

CARRiER OPTiONS

AMERICAN QUEEN RIVERBOAT COMPANY

Take a paddle wheeler or steamboat down the Mississippi River, where you have your pick of over a dozen themed trips, including Antebellum South, '50s and '60s music, quilting and Southern food. These large ships are where you'll find Broadway-esque revues or rollicking cabarets.

AMERICAN CRUISE LINES

Trips on the paddle wheeler *Queen of the West* along the Columbia and Snake rivers follow the path of the Lewis and Clark Expedition amid the beautiful Pacific Northwest scenery – they even run itineraries that specialise in the region's wine.

ST LAWRENCE CRUISE LINES

Many of the major oceangoing cruise lines operate on the expansive St Lawrence, but the family-owned St Lawrence Cruise Line's Victorian reproduction steamboat, the *Canadian Empress*, houses just 36 cabins. The views climbing up the 45-foot-tall locks in the St Lawrence International Seaway can't be beat from a small ship. Entertainment is wholesome Victoriana – think shuffleboard and Big Band tunes.

HiGHLiGHT

Want to see fall foliage but don't want to battle the crowds in Vermont or New Hampshire? Let New England have all the fame (and traffic jams), because the upper Mississippi and St Lawrence Seaway feature some of North America's most brilliant autumn colours. Cruise past gently rolling hills and mountainsides covered in brilliant reds, oranges and yellows. Plus, on a St Lawrence cruise, you just might spot a moose, bear or even a fjord from the small ships that head up to Saguenay Fjord National Park.

Epic Cruise Experiences

Spot alligators in the bayou and blackwater swamps of Cajun country outside New Orleans.

—

Experience the Mississippi with Mark Twain himself . . . or at least a historically accurate docent.

—

Wine and dine on the best farm-to-table cuisine with the grand Multnomah Falls as your backdrop on the Columbia and Snake rivers.

—

Spot beluga whales at play while visiting the Saguenay Fjord National Park on the gulf of the St Lawrence River.

Memphis – covers a bit of both.

The St Lawrence River originates in Lake Ontario and skirts the boundary between the United States and Canada as it flows towards the Atlantic Ocean. It traverses over 744 miles between the cosmopolitan cities of Montreal and Quebec City, moving past lighthouses, national parks and quaint island villages into the Gulf of St Lawrence. The Seaway contains 15 locks that allow for the constant flow of vessels between the Great Lakes and the Atlantic, for both business and pleasure.

The wild and scenic Columbia River Gorge on the Washington-Oregon border is just the thing for the active cruiser. Besides Portland and quirky Astoria, Oregon, most of its sights are about taking in the nature of the river's surrounding valley, visiting Native American fishing platforms and the many local vineyards. Entertainment might include a naturalist lecture about spawning salmon or a tasting of Williamette Valley Pinot Noirs with a professional sommelier.

Below: Beale Street in Memphis;
The Mississippi River;
Right: A paddle wheel steamer

Key Port Feature

NEW ORLEANS

Fried alligator and shrimp jambalaya, voodoo rituals and Mardi Gras traditions, Creole cottages and wrought-iron balconies: New Orleans, Louisiana has one of the most unique cultures of anywhere in the United States. Start with a beignet at Café du Monde, buy a handmade Mardi Gras mask in the French Quarter and end the day at a sultry jazz club. Fancy a bit of Big Easy architecture? Leave the French Quarter for the sumptuous Garden District, or stroll among New Orleans' ghosts in the city's aboveground cemeteries.

WHO'S IT FOR

Did you love history class? How about botany or literature? Then you're going to adore the onboard historians and naturalists, not to mention the Mark Twain impersonator on many Mississippi cruises. While Columbia River cruises can be quite physically active with hiking and biking, passengers usually take Mississippi and St Lawrence cruises to enjoy gentle but excursion-rich days. With fewer passengers to cover costs, river cruise lines are more expensive, but the intimacy with the landscape and fellow passengers is exactly what the more mature or well-heeled passengers love about them. While European riverboats are becoming more family-friendly, North American river cruises rarely have specific amenities or activities for children.

Itinerary

10 DAYS
Oceangoing vessels on the dramatic St Lawrence River head out of Montreal and stop in Quebec City, Halifax, Nova Scotia and even Newfoundland. This cruise can be taken either round-trip from Montreal over a few extra days, or you can take a quick plane trip to Montreal from Boston or New York City.

22 DAYS
With a little over three weeks, you can experience the full majesty of the Mississippi on a trip that follows the mighty river through ten states all the way from New Orleans, Louisiana to St Paul, Minnesota.

THE CRUISE HANDBOOK

LIFESAVER TIP

PACK A PAIR OF WATERPROOF
BINOCULARS MAKE THE
MOST OF YOUR WILDLIFE
SPOTTING IN THE AMAZON
AND GALAPAGOS
ISLANDS.

○ Adventure
○ Outdoors
○ Culture

SOUTH AMERICA

South American cruise destinations offer the stuff of legends, with their whirling dins of birds, insects and wild animals in the world's largest river system – connecting you to the powerful life force of the Amazonian jungle. You can also follow Darwin's footsteps in the Galapagos or take in the majestic glacial fjords of Patagonia.

Cruising in South America is one of the most bucket-list heavy destinations out there. Take in the awe-inspiring biodiversity of the Galapagos Islands and the Amazon jungle, stop for authentic tango in Buenos Aires after taking in the Panama Canal and Cape Horn, and detour to visit the Incan Empire along the way.

With four days to one week, you can experience Patagonia, the Amazon or the Galapagos on a smaller expedition vessel, while the larger cruise lines run a variety of two-week itineraries out of Miami, Buenos Aires or Santiago. These typically will either go through the Panama Canal to the north or around Cape Horn to the south, allowing for a glimpse of Patagonia.

Overland cruisetour excursions to Machu Picchu or Iguazu Falls can round out a traditional cruise that transits between Buenos Aires or Rio de Janeiro and Santiago. Get the most out of your experience by taking advantage of what's offered on board without the hassle of arranging logistics yourself (though you'll spend more than if doing it yourself). That said, it's in the destinations that can't be experienced fully without a boat that South American cruises shine brightest.

Amazon cruises typically

Left: Kayaking in Patagonia's Torres del Paine National Park; **Above:** A blue-footed booby in the Galapagos

153

The unique plant life found in the Amazon Basin may hold many curative properties, including the cure for cancer. During your excursions, local guides point out medicinal plant species and their uses: the roots of the wasai tree for kidney health, lapacho for cancer treatments, cordoncillo is a natural antiseptic and tawari tree bark fights infections. One of the most infamous Amazon plants is used by Peruvian shamans to brew the hallucinogen ayahuasca as spiritual medicine.

start in either Manaus, Brazil, or Iquitos, Peru and last anywhere from three to ten days. To see it all, a six-day cruise is more than enough time. You can take in the sights and sounds of the rainforest on anything from a 12-cabin schooner, a boutique-style wood-sided clipper or larger 140-plus passenger cruise liner, going as upscale or affordable as your budget dictates. This is a biological powerhouse, the last great frontier on Earth, and home to places so remote that there are

Above: Torres del Paine National Park; Right: A Galapagos tortoise

still people here living life exactly as they have for centuries. Along the river you will have the chance to swim with pink river dolphins, spot three-toed sloths, caiman and possibly manatees. The culture of the Amazon is another highlight. Some cruises offer "authentic" Indigenous village experiences, where locals take off their Nikes and cell phones to dress up as they did in the not-too-recent past, though it's really

CARRIER OPTIONS

AUSTRALIS
This Chilean-owned expedition cruise company operating in Patagonia runs sailings year-round and specialises in traversing the fjords.

CELEBRITY CRUISES
Running some of the largest and best-known cruises in the region, Celebrity ships hold up to 98 passengers and, as luxury liners, are perfect for cruisers accustomed to the typical cruise amenities. Like other cruise lines in their tier, their naturalist guides are what park delegates consider

a "Level 3" with at least six years experience.

PUERTO MASUSA FERRY
Locals in the Amazon use ferry transit, so why not you? These boats lack nearly all the creature comforts of the big cruises, but the trip more than makes up for it in a unique experience. From Iquitos, you can hop on three- to seven-day ferry rides both up and downriver. Hammock space costs just around US$100 for the trip. Or you can go "luxury" with a sardine-can cabin for an additional 20 bucks.

Scuba dive the waters around Wolf and Darwin Islands. By booking a dive liveaboard to these submerged volcanoes, you can explore the largest biomass of sharks in the world.

—

Visit Patagonia's mighty Glacier Alley. Whether you see Skua Glacier in the Southern Patagonian Ice Field or take a short three-day cruise in Argentina's Los Glaciares National Park, you won't soon forget the views.

—

Meet a Galapagos tortoise! Get to know the giant tortoises and learn about efforts for their preservation at the Charles Darwin Research Station in Puerto Ayora on Santa Cruz Island, or at the Arnaldo Tupiza Giant Tortoise Breeding Center on Isabela Island.

WHO'S IT FOR

With partial circum-navigations of the continent on offer alongside stunning routes in Patagonia, the Amazon and the Galapagos, South American cruises are ideal for nature-lovers and adventurers who wish to experience a wide range of cultures and ecosystems.

just as fun to head off to visit the small communities that live here.

On a Patagonia or Cape Horn cruise passing Punta Arenas, you will have the chance to take an expedition to Magdalena Island, home to Chile's largest colony of Magellanic penguins. If you're headed to the Galapagos Islands, cruises will take you to regions of the park that are too far for day trips from a land base. If you can, aim for an eight-day itinerary that will make the most of your travel time to the archipelago (remember, you'll have to fly here from either Quito or Guayaquil). With cruises in the Galapagos Islands offering incredibly skilled naturalist guides as a matter of course, you'll be able to get the most out of what you see along the way.

Cruises in any of these regions – the Galapagos Islands, the Amazon river basin, and Patagonia – give access to a world that otherwise remains out of reach. With the help of onboard naturalists, they'll take you up close to some of the wildest zones on the planet.

Right: A view of Machu Picchu

Key Port Feature

MANAUS

Manaus is the largest city in the Amazon – a port city that needs no ocean. You can spend a few half-days exploring one of its open-air markets or visiting the botanical parks and gardens. Also worthwhile is a trip out to the Museu do Seringal Vila Paraíso. Located on a former rubber estate, this museum gives great historical insight into the gilded era of rubber barons. Afterwards, take a picnic out to the Praia da Lua, the best beach in Manaus.

IQUITOS

For a less touristic place to roam – and about a million times smaller – Iquitos, Peru has a great little riverside walkway, where you can snack on alligator-like caiman steaks while watching the world go by and getting a taste of local life.

Itinerary

3 DAYS

Ideal for backpackers, the Navimag ferry trip lacks the bells and whistles of a luxury cruise through the same waters, but the price tag makes it a much more affordable way to travel through the heart of Chilean Patagonia from Puerto Montt to Puerto Natales.

10 DAYS

Since Peru's Pacaya Samiria is about 100 miles southwest of Iquitos, it takes a while to get there. Ten-day itineraries include exploration along the Amazon, Marañón and Ucayali Rivers, daily wilderness hikes, boat excursions to check out the small waterways, as well as nighttime hikes. En route, stop at villages to buy handicrafts, visit with locals and sample the unique foods and drinks of the Amazon.

NOTES

NOTES

NOTES

iNDEX

ABOUT THE AUTHORS

MICHELLE BARAN

Michelle Baran is a senior editor at *Travel Weekly*, where she has been covering the travel industry since 2007. Baran also co-authored the *Frommer's EasyGuide to River Cruising*. Previously, she covered the fashion industry at Conde Nast's *Footwear News*. She received her Masters in Journalism from Northwestern University.

RAY BARTLETT

Ray Bartlett has written numerous guidebooks for Lonely Planet. His debut novel, *Sunsets of Tulum*, was a Midwest Book Review fiction selection, and a new novel, *The Vasemaker's Daughter*, is forthcoming spring 2019. His hobbies include surfing and Argentine tango.

GREG BENCHWICK

Greg has been exploring by water since he was a little boy. Since then, Greg's written dozens of Lonely Planet books, interviewed heads-of-state and Grammy-award winners, and cruised some of the planet's most beautiful waterways.

ALEX LEVITON

Alex Leviton is a long-time Lonely Planet writer (*Italy; Happy; The Caribbean*) who grew up on a peninsula, lived on a ship for four months, and travels by water — cruises, sailboats, kayaks, Canadian canoes, Turkish gulets — whenever she can.

EMILY MATCHAR

Emily Matchar is a writer based in Hong Kong (mostly) and Pittsboro, North Carolina (sometimes). She writes about travel, culture, science, technology, social issues and more for magazines and newspapers, and has contributed to several dozen Lonely Planet books.

BRENDAN SAINSBURY

Brendan has been traveling, researching and writing for Lonely Planet since 2005. He has co-authored three books about Alaska, a region he loves for its wild trails, placid paddling, eccentric off-the-grid communities, and rugged frontier spirit.

SARAH STOCKING

Sarah Stocking is the California and Mexico destination editor at Lonely Planet. Prior to landing her dream job at LP she helped people plan trips to the polar regions. Always up for an adventure, kayaking with minke whales in Whilemmina Bay is her favorite one yet.

BRANDON PRESSER

Author of the Smoooth Sailing, Planning, and Inspiration sections of this book, Brandon's most memorable seafaring journey is a voyage to Pitcairn Island by cargo freighter. Brandon is also a PADI Divemaster, enjoying the wildlife under the waves as much as the culture on land. He has an apartment in New York City that collects a lot of dust while he's out on assignment for Bloomberg, Travel+Leisure, and his American television show, *Tour Group*.

TIANA TEMPLEMAN

Dr Tiana Templeman is a Brisbane-based travel author, award-winning freelance journalist, radio presenter and media industry academic. She writes about all things travel related for Australian and international newspapers, magazines and websites. Cruising is one of her favourite ways to see the world.

Published in January 2019 by Lonely Planet Global Ltd
CRN 554153
www.lonelyplanet.com
ISBN 978 1 788681032
© Lonely Planet 2019
© Photographs as indicated 2019
Printed in China

Managing Director, Publishing Piers Pickard
Associate Publisher Robin Barton
Commissioning Editor Nora Rawn
Art Director Katharine Van Itallie
Print production Nigel Longuet

Written by Michelle Baran, Ray Bartlett, Greg Benchwick, Alex Leviton, Emily Matchar, Brandon Presser, Brendan Sainsbury, Sarah Stocking, and Dr. Tiana Templeman.

Cover illustration by Niki Fisher

STAY IN TOUCH lonelyplanet.com/contact

AUSTRALIA The Malt Store, Level 3, 551 Swanston St, Carlton, Victoria 3053 T: 03 8379 8000

IRELAND Digital Depot, Roe Lane (off Thomas St) The Digital Hub, Dublin 8, D08 TCV4

USA 124 Linden St, Oakland, CA 94607
T: 510 250 6400

UK 240 Blackfriars Rd, London SE1 8NW
T: 020 3771 5100

Paper in this book is certified against the Forest Stewardship Council™ standards. FSC™ promotes environmentally responsible, socially beneficial and economically viable management of the world's forests.